penny candy

JONATHAN NORTON

penny candy

• a confection •

DEEP VELLUM PUBLISHING
DALLAS, TEXAS

Deep Vellum Publishing
3000 Commerce St., Dallas, Texas 75226
deepvellum.org · @deepvellum

Deep Vellum is a 501c3 nonprofit literary arts organization
founded in 2013 with the mission to bring
the world into conversation through literature.

First edition, 2021

Support for this publication has been provided in part by the Addy Foundation,
the Moody Fund for the Arts, and Amazon Literary Partnership.

ISBNs: 978-1-64605-105-2 (paperback) | 978-1-64605-106-9 (ebook)

LIBRARY OF CONGRESS CONTROL NUMBER: 2021946199

Front cover design by Justin Childress | justinchildress.co

Interior Layout and Typesetting by KGT

PRINTED IN THE UNITED STATES OF AMERICA

For Laura Mae and Willie James Norton

PRODUCTION HISTORY

penny candy was commissioned by the Dallas Theater Center (Kevin Moriarty, artistic director; Jeffrey Woodward, managing director) and had its world premiere there on June 12, 2019. The production was directed by Derrick Sanders. The set design was by Courtney O'Neill, the costume design by Samantha C. Jones, the lighting design by Alan C. Edwards, the sound design and original music were by Elisheba Ittoop, the hair and makeup design were by Cherelle Guyton, the video design was by Sarah Harris, the prop design was by John Slauson, and the fight choreography was by Ashley H. White. The assistant director was Ashley Roberson and the stage managers were Anna Baranski and Samantha Honeycutt.

The cast was:

Dubba J	Leon Addison Brown
Laura Mae	Liz Mikel
Jon-Jon	Esau Price
Kingston	Ace Anderson
Rose	Claudia Logan
Nicole	Tiana Kaye Blair
Donnie	Jamal Sterling

penny candy was developed with the support of PlayPenn in Philadelphia, Pennsylvania.

CHARACTERS

JON-JON – African American, twelve years old. Helps his dad with the family business.

DUBBA J – African American, sixty-two. Retired. He now runs the family business—the neighborhood candy house. Dubba J's real name is Willie James, but folks call him WJ, which often sounds like Dubba J.

KINGSTON – Jamaican, late twenties. Crack dealer. He works out of the apartment next door to the candy house. He's adopted Dubba J, Laura Mae, and Jon-Jon as his family.

LAURA MAE – African American, late forties to early fifties. Jon-Jon's mom and Dubba J's wife. She started the candy house and ran it for many years before her husband retired. Now she works as a nurses' aide in a nursing home.

ROSE – African American, early twenties. Crack dealer. She works for Kingston. She grew up in the neighborhood and the candy house has always been her second home.

NICOLE – African American, mid to late twenties. A single mom of a four-year-old girl. Like Rose, she grew up in the neighborhood. She leads the Neighborhood Watch.

DONNIE – African American, early to mid-forties. He and his wife are close friends of Dubba J and Laura Mae. He's looking for his son, who is missing.

SETTING

A candy house in Pleasant Grove, a working-class neighborhood in Dallas. The candy house is a mom and pop store operated out of a one-bedroom apartment.

TIME

Summertime, 1988.

NOTE: A "/" indicates when dialogue is cut off and jumped on by the next person.

ENTER JON-JON

I guess I should start with the question playwrights always get. How long did it take to write the play? The process for *penny candy* started in the summer of 2015 when I was commissioned to write a new play for DTC.

The months passed, and by early fall I was still play-less. I had plenty of ideas, but the only idea that really interested me was one I'd had a few years prior but never started. It was *penny candy* . . . or a play sorta like *penny candy*—then called *candyland*. It was about a childless couple based on my parents who ran a candy house. It was basically *The Wire* meets *Homicide: Life on the Streets*—really dark, graphic, and sad. But something didn't feel right.

Remember that I said in *candyland* my parents did not have children? Weird, right? Well that was because I could not put myself inside that world. Because that was not the world I remembered. It wasn't my truth. That wasn't my childhood. And I began to wonder why I'd want to remember my parents that way. That wasn't their story either. The tone of the play began to shift in my mind and EUREKA—not only did I have a new play—but I got to join my parents onstage. Enter Jon-Jon!

Another EUREKA moment came when I found a beautiful book by the photographer Jamel Shabazz, titled *A Time Before Crack*. Jamel's book celebrates beautiful expressions of love, brotherhood/sisterhood, community/solidarity, black joy . . . a time before crack. His later books examined the horrific aftermath of crack on African American communities. I decided to explore this further in *penny candy*. My play follows a family and community at a turning point. The innocence of yesterday hangs in the balance, while a dangerous and uncertain future awaits. The story is hilarious, heartening, and haunting in equal measure.

So back to the question I posed earlier. I started writing *penny candy* in 2015. I submitted the final rehearsal draft in February 2019. Four years. But in truth, I've been writing this play my entire life.

ABOUT THE CANDY HOUSE:

The candy house is operated out of a one-bedroom apartment right smack dab in the middle of a badly aging apartment complex that has seen better days.

There are two doors. A regular front door and a sliding glass door on another wall. The front door is always locked. Only the family uses that door. Customers use the sliding glass door. There are burglar bars on both doors.

The candy house is organized in this way: there is a glass showcase counter containing a big mix of different candies. Behind the counter is a long folding table that contains even more candy. Also on this table is a jar of dill and sour pickles, pickled pigs feet, and two racks of potato chips, popcorn, etc. All the candies are in their colorful merchandise boxes from the wholesale supply store.

Above the candy table, on the wall is a sign made of multiple pieces of construction paper that reads, "THE WALL OF FAME." The wall is covered with framed pictures of children, families, and neighborhood functions, pool parties, and birthdays. There are certificates on the wall that say "Buckner Bees" and a few report cards, too. There is a wooden plaque of two hearts combined that reads "Love Is James and Laura."

The kitchen is the kind with an open bar that allows you to see through.

Now—without getting into too much elaborate detail that will flummox the set designer—somewhere in the room there is a:

Second refrigerator in addition to the fridge in the kitchen. This is the "business fridge." A tiny TV area.

There is a nacho/frito pie and snow cone station and it should not be close to the candy counter or table. Three folding chairs. Two by the sliding glass door and one by the TV area.

As audience members find their seats, they see JON-JON *engrossed in a cheap, bootleg VHS of Berry Gordy's* The Last Dragon. *"Who's The Master? Sho-nuff!" He eats Tony the Tiger Kellogg's Frosted Flakes straight out the box. He chases the cereal down with Tahitian Treat fruit punch.*

The volume is turned down low on the video. But none of that matters. JON-JON *knows every word, gesture and karate chop—which he takes great joy in reenacting when the spirit moves him.*

After a while he gets bored with the movie and turns it off. His father, DUBBA J, *is laid out on a pallet on the floor. But he can't sleep. His eyes wide open with worry. He tries to sleep but it ain't working for him.*

The kitchen light is on. The only other light comes from the TV and a plastic camp light near DUBBA J*'s head.*

A minute before the play starts, a noise is heard outside. DUBBA J*'s body pops up. Quiet for a beat.* DUBBA J *lies back down.*

JON-JON *turns the TV back on to catch the WFAA Channel 8 News. The meteorologist drones on about a heat wave.*

Then another noise.

ACT ONE – SCENE ONE

Scene: DUBBA J *jumps up. He gestures for* JON-JON *to turn down the volume.* DUBBA J *creeps to the blinds and looks out. He hears something coming from the back room. He takes a big swig of beer and heads back to check it out.*

JON-JON *takes a swig of beer when his father is gone.*

On the TV, the words "SHOOT-OUT IN PLEASANT GROVE" appear on the screen, and then footage of crime scene tape and police officers at a swimming pool as dusk settles.

> JON-JON
>
> Daddy! Daddy! DADDY!
> DADDY COME HEEEEEEEERE!!!

DUBBA J *comes running out of the bedroom.*

> DUBBA J
>
> JON-JON!

> JON-JON
>
> We're on TV!

> DUBBA J
>
> Boy don't scare me like that!

On the screen we see a bunch of kids in swimsuits standing outside an apartment. Another group of kids stands inside the apartment. A sign on the sliding glass door reads "We're Open." A teenage girl is being interviewed on the patio by the sliding glass door.

JON-JON

Look! It's the candy house! That's us!

Ooooooh, it's the twins! Binky and Twinky! Shoot, Binky look real big on TV.

There is a loud banging at the sliding glass door.

KINGSTON

Open the door. Somebody open the bloodclaat door.

(More banging)

Pupa!

Open the door. I will tear the bars off with my bare hands. Pupa!

*(*DUBBA J *opens the sliding glass door.* KINGSTON *rushes into the candy house)*

Who in here with you? Somebody back there?

*(*KINGSTON *lifts his shirt to reveal a a big-ass hunting knife strapped to his waist. He grips the handle. He searches the apartment. Room by room. Then he comes back out)*

I don't see nobody. What the fuck was bredda screaming for?

JON-JON

Because we're on TV.

KINGSTON

The bloodclaat TV got you screaming like a lagga head gyal?

DUBBA J

Now Kingston, you know I got nothing but respect for you. But I'm gonna need you to speak full and complete English when you got something to say 'bout my boy.

KINGSTON

Pupa, just tell brother not to scream like that nuh muh. You know what go through muh mind?

DUBBA J

We didn't mean to scare you.

KINGSTON

Do I look scared to you?

DUBBA J

Oh noooooooooooo.

KINGSTON

I was just being a concerned neighbor. Anyting wrong with that?
(Now on TV there is footage of a group of women huddled together, crying. JON-JON stares at the screen. Fixated. KINGSTON hurries over and turns off the TV)
And cut this shit off. Don't wan' see no more. Not good for Jon-Jon psyche.
(Beat)
Brother, weh yaw seh?

JON-JON

Everyting criss.
DUBBA J doesn't know what they're saying.

Eh?

JON-JON

Mi a chat di truut.

KINGSTON

Look at you.

JON-JON

Mi di tap a di tap.

DUBBA J *is downright confused.*

KINGSTON

You look tired, pupa. You and brother should go home.

JON-JON

We tried to go home but the police made us come back inside.

DUBBA J

Police said there was a curfew till morning. Our ass stuck right here, looks like.

KINGSTON

Fuck dem bloodclaat curfew. This used to be such a nice neighborhood. Good, quiet place to do business. Nobody fuck with nobody. Everybody keep to themselves. Now here the gangs come and there goes the fucking neighborhood. That shit at the swimming pool was a gang shooting. The gangs them did dat.

JON-JON

Gangs?

KINGSTON

From California. They call themselves the Bloods. They've taken
over Bruton Terrace. And Sycene Road. And we're next. Ragga-
muffins. I won't stand for this. They are a cancer. But I am the
cure.

JON-JON

It's gonna be a long, hot summer. And now everybody afraid to go
to the swimming pool.

KINGSTON

You fuck with a swimming pool in the middle of the Texas summer, you fuck with me. Can't believe this shit. Yesterday it was like
Walnut Grove or some shit. Now we got the news cameras and a
bloodclaat police curfew. That's how it always starts.

JON-JON

Walnut Grove like on *Little House on the Prairie*? Wait! You watch
Little House on the—

KINGSTON

And what the fuck is wrong with that? It's good TV, with enter-
taining storylines, and interesting characters who remind you of
people you know.
(JON-JON *finds this oh-so funny*)
Pupa make him stop laughing. Ya tek bad tings for joke?
(*They stop laughing*)

Nothing funny. You lose everyting you work for. Nothing funny 'bout dat. Am I missing something?

JON-JON

Hush, Kingston.

DUBBA J

Boy!

JON-JON

It means sorry in Patois. Hush.

DUBBA J

Hush. Hush.

A beat passes.

KINGSTON

Hush. Hush. Mi did see writing pon the wall. Time to pay the price. Pupa, I fucked up. I really fucked up. Mi para. Para.

DUBBA J

Awww boy, don't beat yourself up. So you had a shitty-ass day. Sometimes a whole goddamn year can be shitty-ass. So one shitty-ass day ain't shit. Let the muthafucka come. Then let the muthafucka go. And that girl gonna be fine. She was just shot in the leg. The kids say she was talking and alert and in her right mind when they put her in that ambulance. Take it easy on yourself.

KINGSTON

I don't like the shooting. It's getting too close, pupa. Too close.

DUBBA J

Well that was the cancer. But you the cure. Ain't that what you said?

KINGSTON

You right, pupa. You always right.

DUBBA J

Goddammit, I know I'm right.
    (They laugh)
Now sit your ass down and relax a spell. You're the guest of honor. Jon-Jon, get the man a beer for his troubles. Kingston, let me show my 'preciation.

KINGSTON

No, man, I'm working. Don't drink when I work. Keep the right head. You should do the same, pupa. But I'll have a snow cone.

DUBBA J

What flavor do you want?

KINGSTON

Surprise me.

DUBBA J

Jon-Jon, make your special concoction. Jon-Jon got this concoction he makes where he mixes all the flavors together.

JON-JON

All eight of 'em.

Nothing about this sounds appealing to KINGSTON.

DUBBA J

And then he adds some Diet Cherry 7UP.

JON-JON

That Diet Cherry 7UP is what sets it off.

DUBBA J

You'd think it tastes like shit. But it's some kind of wonderful.

JON-JON

It's the 7UP. I'm trying to tell you.

DUBBA J

Jon-Jon stop talking and show the man. And make it an extra-large.

JON-JON

Extra-large coming up!

JON-JON *starts on the snow cone. Putting ice in the grinder.*

DUBBA J

You want some chicken? Made some special. Just for you. With that spicy sauce you like. Yeah?

KINGSTON *shrugs his shoulders.*

KINGSTON

Pupa.

KINGSTON shows his ring finger.

DUBBA J

Now you ain't gotta be all ugly! If you don't want the chicken. Just say you don't want the goddamn chicken.

KINGSTON

No. Pupa. Your ring finger.
(KINGSTON *chuckles*)
It ain't turned green yet, has it?

DUBBA J

No. But it itches like a muthafucka. You working on it?

KINGSTON notices JON-JON *is being nosy.*

KINGSTON

(to JON-JON*)*
Eh. You be nosy.
Turn it around and do your job.

DUBBA J

You hear that?

KINGSTON

Wah gwaan?

There is some ruckus outside.

(He goes to the sliding glass door)

It's them damn television news people again. Right under the street light. They talking to somebo—ahhhh shit!!!

                    KINGSTON

Wah gwaan?

                    DUBBA J

You stay yo ass right here.

>   DUBBA J *opens up the sliding glass door and hurries outside.* KINGSTON *peeps out.*

                    KINGSTON

Raasclaat!

                    JON-JON

Wat a guh dung?

                    KINGSTON

Mary! Jesus! Joseph!

                    JON-JON

Wah gwaan? Bumbo Pussy Claat!!!

>   LAURA MAE *rushes past* KINGSTON *and into the candy house. She's dressed for bed. Her hair is wrapped up for the night. She wears the*

first robe and slippers she could find. Nothing matches. This is not
LAURA MAE*'s finest fashion hour.* DUBBA J *hurries in behind her. He*
locks up.

LAURA MAE	JON-JON
Where is my baby / Jon-Jon!	Mama!

Mother and son embrace.

LAURA MAE

Mama's here, baby! Mama is here!
Something told me when I left here I should take you home with
me. I should've followed my first mind. Lord, I should've listened!

DUBBA J	LAURA MAE
Girl, what the hell done / got into you?	I had to come see 'bout my baby.

DUBBA J

The boy is fine. If you just woulda called / first—

LAURA MAE

Dubba J, I tried to call but the line kept being busy.

JON-JON

All the kids was using the phone to call their parents.

LAURA MAE

And didn't nobody think to call me?

DUBBA J

Laura Mae, it was a sho-nuff mad house.

LAURA MAE

That ain't a good enough excuse. One minute! One minute! Was
all it would take. Pick up the phone and call me to say, Laura Mae.
There was a shooting. Jon-Jon is okay. We all okay. Oh and let me
put Jon-Jon on the phone to reassure you because I love you Laura
Mae and that's what a husband does for his wife. He gives her a
goddamn courtesy call.

DUBBA J

Awww, Laura Mae!

LAURA MAE

Awwwww, Laura Mae nothing. I didn't know shit had happened
until Tracy Rowlett popped up on my television screen with breaking news. Shoot-out in Pleasant Grove.

DUBBA J

See now. Now they's wrong. It wasn't / no shoot-out.

LAURA MAE

And I saw these apartments on TV and that just did me in! And that's
when I went down on my knees! Praying for my child. And I heard my
Heavenly Father speak to me. The Lord said, "Laura Mae! Get your
ass out this muthafuckin' house and go see 'bout your child."

KINGSTON

Language, mommy.

(She finally notices KINGSTON)

I don't like it when ladies curse.

LAURA MAE

I speak how I please. And your ass shouldn't be here no how. Dubba J, what is he doing here?

KINGSTON

Mommy, wah gwaan?

LAURA MAE

Speak English?

JON-JON

He said, "what's going on?"

LAURA MAE

How do you know what he's saying?
Go to the back room. Don't come out till I call you.
    (JON-JON *trudges off to the back room)*
Dubba J, I asked you a question.

KINGSTON

Mommy . . . ?

LAURA MAE

And I'm not your goddamn mama. Don't call me that shit no more.

Tree (three) hours ago, you call me Pumpkin and kiss me on me cheek. Now you talk to me crazy. Wah gwaan?

LAURA MAE

You have something to do with that girl that got shot?

KINGSTON

What you take me for?

LAURA MAE

Dubba J, I don't want him around Jon-Jon ever again.

KINGSTON

Wah gwaan? I come here being a good neighbor. Pupa! Talk to mommy!

DUBBA J

Now Laura Mae, you can't ask for a better neighbor than this man right here.

LAURA MAE

He's a gang leader!

KINGSTON

Do I look like a gang leader to you? Look at mi shirt. Look at mi shoes.

DUBBA J

The boy's pants are pressed and everything. You looking at a businessman.

KINGSTON

That's right. Me a businessman.

DUBBA J

We businessmen, Laura Mae. I got a business. He got a business.
We got common interests.

KINGSTON

We Men of Commerce. Ain't that right, pupa?

LAURA MAE

You are a DRUG DEAL-ER.

KINGSTON

That's what I said. I'm a businessman.

LAURA MAE

Get out of my house.

KINGSTON

Mommy!

LAURA MAE

Call me that word one more time.

KINGSTON   LAURA MAE
But mom / my . . .   What I say?

KINGSTON *is speechless. A beat. Then he storms out the candy house,
leaving the sliding glass door wide open.* DUBBA J *hurries and locks up.*

DUBBA J

Laura Mae, you getting out of hand.

LAURA MAE

I don't want him around my baby after what happened tonight.
And you know how I feel about those boys on the corner.

DUBBA J

Kingston, ain't one of them boys on the corner. The boys on the
corner work for him. He keeps the boys on the corner in line.
Kingston keep the peace 'round here. You know that.

LAURA MAE

Yeah? He keep the peace?
How come that girl just got shot? Huh? Oh but he keep the peace.
Turned this place into Dodge City. That's what he did. Shoot-outs
in the street.

DUBBA J

Awwww hell, Cookie! You see one little thing on TV and 'bout just
lose your goddamn mind. Talking to people crazy and shit and you
ain't even got all the facts.

LAURA MAE

Shoot-out in Pleasant Grove. How would you react? And my baby
in the middle of it.

DUBBA J

First off it wasn't no shoot-out. They just said that shit to get you
to watch. A shoot-out is when it's two people shooting back and

forth. This was just one person shooting. One person. One shooting. That all it was. Feel better now?

> LAURA MAE

No! No. I don't feel better. A shooting is a shooting. You can't sugarcoat that shit. Don't matter how many times it happen. One shooting! One shooting is enough. Dubba J, I can't believe you fixed your mouth to say that. Shot that poor innocent baby down like a dog in the street. That's what matters.

> *A beat.*

> DUBBA J

Laura Mae, you right. I'm sorry.
>   *(Another beat)*
I didn't mean it that way.
>   *(Another beat. She doesn't respond)*
Cookie . . . ?

> LAURA MAE

Do we know the girl? She come to the candy house?

> DUBBA J

Don't think so. The kids say she was visiting her granny.

> LAURA MAE

We know her granny?

> DUBBA J

Naw. She live 'cross the way in Las Lomas Apartments.

How old was she?

(*A beat.* DUBBA J *doesn't want to answer*)

Willie James?

DUBBA J

'bout Jon-Jon age.

LAURA MAE

My Lord, my Lord. I can't. I just can't.

LAURA MAE *finds a chair and crumbles into it.*

DUBBA J

Cookie, stop worrying yourself. The baby was shot in the leg. She gonna be fine. And—and—and Mama Eula was there. She said it was a car she never seen before. Just rolled up and started shooting. It was some fools that don't even live here that did that shit. Kingston's boys ain't got nothing to do with that. Things ain't all bad like you thinking. And the police is on it. The police swooped right up in here. Hell they on it. We ain't got to worry.

LAURA MAE

The police? Yeah?

That supposed to make me feel better?

(*Without turning her head to look at* JON-JON)

Jon-Jon, what I say?

(*Maybe she really does have eyes in the back of her head.* JON-JON

goes back in the bedroom)

I don't feel good about the candy house anymore. I don't feel safe.

Never thought I'd say those words. Dubba J, I want—

(DUBBA J *plants a sweet kiss on her lips. He holds her in his arms*)

Willie James, what you do some crazy shit like that for?

DUBBA J

Awwwwwwww come on, Cookie. Come on, it's gonna be okay. Let me hold you, Cookie. Let me make everything better.

LAURA MAE

You know how you can really make everything better, Dubba J?

DUBBA J

Don't you dare say that goddamn Walmart.

LAURA MAE

What's wrong with Walmart? All the retirees work at Walmart. Greet folks when they come through the door. If you really need something to do. Then do that. Didn't Shorty get on at Walmart?

DUBBA J

Shorty hate Walmart. He only started working there 'cause his wife got tired of him bothering her around the house. He hates that place. He tried to give notice three times. But his boss won't let him quit. You know what it's called when you want to quit your job but your boss won't let you go? Slavery.

LAURA MAE

At least I can sleep at night.

DUBBA J

You gonna sleep any better knowing I gave up? I spent forty years of my life making white folks richer. Punching a time clock for their benefit more than mine. And I thought I was really doing something until they gave me a plaque, and some cake and punch and sent me on my way. Then I realized the goddamn joke was on me.

LAURA MAE

They gave you a nice retirement / package—

DUBBA J

Gave. The white folks gave / me—

LAURA MAE

You earned it.

DUBBA J

I want to have my own, Cookie. What's wrong with that? I wanna be the boss of something. Every man gotta be the boss of something at least once in his life or he not a real man. I ain't never been the boss of nothing. But I'm the boss of this candy house right here. I'm sixty-two years old and this is my time. Now or never. I expect you to understand.

(LAURA MAE *gets quiet. She turns away from him*)

You not gonna start crying on me, are you? Awwwwwww, Cookie.

(*He takes his wife in his arms*)

Come on, Cookie, baby. Let me hold you.

LAURA MAE

No. I don't want you hugging and kissing on me. Don't touch me.

Smelling like beer. Jon-Jon, come on!

(JON-JON *comes out of the room*)

We going home. We all going home. Together. Go on Dubba J, take a piss 'fore we get on the road because I know how you do.

(Standoff)

Jon-Jon, tell your daddy to go to the bathroom.

JON-JON

Go take a piss, daddy.

LAURA MAE

Not like that.

(DUBBA J *storms off to the bathroom.* LAURA MAE *goes over to the money box)*

Let's see what your daddy did today. There's over two hundred dollars here. He made this much in one day?

JON-JON

Would have been more if it hadn't been for the shooting.

LAURA MAE

How he make this much money in one day?

JON-JON

The boys on the corner. Every time they come in here they compete for who can spend the most money. One boy spent thirty dollars just on nachos and Frito pies. He was showing off to some girls. And then sometimes Kingston buy up a bunch of stuff for next door. You know, mama, while we on the subject of money. Daddy cut me down to three dollars a day. Eighteen dollars a week.

He said I'm not earning my five dollars a day. But shoot, that's a twelve-dollar loss I'm taking. That's a big cut. Shouldn't he have run that by you first?

LAURA MAE

Your daddy don't run shit by me no more, looks like.

JON-JON

Well you need to get daddy back on track 'cause mama, it's getting rough. You notice I ain't buying my Transformers, and my He-Man, and my Voltrons, and my Thundercats like I used to. The other day, we were at Big Town Mall, I stood outside the Hickory Farms store. Couldn't even afford a cheese ball.

LAURA MAE

Mama gonna take you back to Big Town Mall and buy you all the cheese balls your precious little heart desires. And you ain't gotta work here no more. Mama just gonna give you whatever you want. 'Cause you work hard enough in school.

JON-JON

That right!

LAURA MAE

My baby not gonna want for nothing.

JON-JON

And I can't even get my nachos at KMart like I'm accustomed.

LAURA MAE

(Wrapping her son in her arms)

Oh my poor baby.

The toilet flushes.

There is a knock at the sliding glass door. LAURA MAE *shushes* JON-JON.

Another knock. DUBBA J *comes out of the bathroom.*

DUBBA J

Who is that?

LAURA MAE

(Under her breath)

I don't know.

(DUBBA J moves toward the sliding glass door)

Dubba J!

ROSE

(From outside)

Daddy! Daddy it's me! Rosie-Girl!

LAURA MAE

Dubba J! We going home.

DUBBA J *opens the sliding glass door and lets* ROSE *in the candy house.*

Hey, daddy, Kingston sent me. Say you got some chicken to pick up. Mama, what you doing here? I thought you'd gone home.

LAURA MAE

Why these fools keep calling us mama and daddy? We only got one child.

(JON-JON *proudly raises his hand*)

Right there.

ROSE

Everybody call y'all mama and daddy. Shoot, I been calling y'all mama and daddy since I was Jon-Jon's age.

(Chuckles)

Mama, why you tripping? Hey, daddy, the food ready?

DUBBA J

I got chicken right here.

ROSE *pokes her head over the kitchen counter.*

ROSE

Oooooh, that smells so good. I can't wait. I want a bite.

She runs into the kitchen to nibble on some chicken.

LAURA MAE

We are going home!

ROSE

Mama, I'm hungry. I haven't eaten good all day. I had a worried
feeling all-day-long. Like a premonition or something. Then that
li'l girl got shot, that did a number on me. I mean I thought we had
everything under control.

(Talks while she's nibbling)

Me and Kingston, we try and do right by everybody. Somebody
get outta line—we present them with a very compelling argument
as to why said behavior is not in the best interest of their health
and well-being. And then everybody copacetic. And that's the way
we've always done things. But now some fool wanna start shooting
people. It's a sad day in the neighborhood.

JON-JON

Kingston say this neighborhood used to be like *Little House on the
Prairie*.

ROSE

And it's gonna STAY *Little House on the Prairie*. I'm gonna see to
that. Personally. You gonna be like Half-Pint. Daddy gonna be Pa.

(Points to LAURA MAE*)*

You gonna be Mrs. Oleson.
Say, daddy, you got enough for five beef sandwiches? That be my
lunch and my dinner tomorrow.

DUBBA J

Five?

39

Five. For sho. Square business. And I want three popsicles. The kind with the cream inside. I want an orange, a pink and a green.

DUBBA J

Jon-Jon, we got a customer.

ROSE *reaches into her bra for the money, giving it to* DUBBA J. *He hurries to the kitchen.*

LAURA MAE

Let your daddy do it. It's after ten. You off the clock.
(LAURA MAE *goes to the TV chair and sits down. She MAKES* JON-JON *sit in her lap)*
You sit in your mama's lap. You ain't grown yet.

DUBBA J

I'm the boss of the candy house. Jon-Jon answer to me. Get off your mama lap. I'll give you fifteen dollars.

JON-JON

Yes sir!

LAURA MAE

Twenty-five dollars. Sit your ass back down.

JON-JON *sits back on her lap.*

DUBBA J

Forty dollars.

JON-JON *jumps up.*

LAURA MAE

Forty-five dollars.

He sits down.

DUBBA J

Fifty-five dollars.

He jumps up.

LAURA MAE

Fifty-seven dollars.

He sits back down.

DUBBA J

Fifty-eight dollars.
(*Thinks*)
And a sip of beer.

JON-JON

Sold.

LAURA MAE

Shit.

DUBBA J

Come on, son, help your daddy make this money.

JON-JON *hurries to help.*

LAURA MAE

Money ain't everything. Men of Commerce bullshit. That ain't what the candy house is all about and you know it. Hell, I wasn't even thinking about money when I started the candy house. I started it to keep the babies from getting hit by cars trying to go down the road to the gas station. And then you gonna turn it into something that's all about money. Shame.

DUBBA J

Money is what got us into that big house in Red Oak.

LAURA MAE

It ain't that big.

DUBBA J *stops chopping meat.*

ROSE *tries to change the subject to lessen the tension.*

ROSE

Jon-Jon, make me that special concoction with the Diet Cherry 7UP.

(JON-JON *lights up. He goes to the fridge to get the ice and soda. But his dad gestures for him to come to the kitchen to help*)

Damn, I'm hungry right now, shoot. Let me see what I wanna eat.

(*Goes behind the candy counter*)

Ooooooh, I know just what I want.

ROSE *opens up a sour pickle jar and reaches in.*

LAURA MAE

Girl don't you stick your drug-infested hands in my pickles. Use the damn tongs, shit!

ROSE *takes the tongs and pulls out a pickle. She bites off a quarter of the pickle. Then she takes a package of Cherry Kool-Aid and pours it on top of the pickle. She takes a big bite. The flavor makes her face scrunch up.*

ROSE

Ooooooooooooh. That hit the spot.

(Her beeper goes off)

Who that? Pleaaaaaasseeee. Cheap fool. I don't sell no two-dollar rocks. Who he think I am? The news cameras out. And the police. He crazy.

(She takes another bite)

Mama, why you looking at me like that?

LAURA MAE

Such a shame. You had so much potential.

ROSE

Awwwwwww, mama. Don't start in on me again.

LAURA MAE *points to a picture of* ROSE *in her high school cap and gown.*

LAURA MAE

See that girl on that wall. That baby had something going for her. That's the Rosie-Girl I know.

Daddy, make her stop.

LAURA MAE

Candy Man don't run me.

(LAURA MAE *gives him a look. He shakes his head like, "No, I certainly do not"*)

And every time I lay eyes on you I'm gonna tell you what I think, till you get some sense in that head of yours. Don't like it, then don't bring your ass up in the candy house no more.

(Beat)

Shit you need to listen to me. Nicole listened to me. Got her shit together real good.

ROSE

Mama—

Please stop comparing me to other people.

LAURA MAE

Dubba J, finish this girl's shit up. So we can get the hell up outta here.

(*Quiet. No one talks for awhile.* ROSE *has lost interest in the pickle.* DUBBA J *and* JON-JON *finish up the sandwiches.* LAURA MAE*'s attention goes back to the picture on the wall*)

An honest job. So many options.

ROSE

Mama!

(Beat)

Options? I worked at Skaggs Alpha Beta in produce. I sprayed fruits and vegetables with a water hose. Then I got laid off.

                         LAURA MAE
Levines?

                           ROSE
I hated Levines.

                         LAURA MAE
They made you manager.

                           ROSE
Of the lay-away. Big deal. Just one department.

                         LAURA MAE
It was a big deal. The manager of the lay-away is always the most feared person in the whole damn store. Nobody fucks with the manager of the lay-away. Piss them off and all your shit be GONE. GONE. Your kids don't have no back-to-school clothes. No Christmas presents. No Easter outfits. No nothing.
    (JON-JON *goes to the snow cone machine to start pouring ice in the machine*)
All your shit GONE. And half your money, too. That's one person you don't fuck around with. Everybody know that.
    (JON-JON *starts crushing ice. The machine is LOUD.* LAURA MAE *talks over it*)
AND YOU HAD ALL THAT POWER AND—JON-JON! YOU HEAR ME TALKING!
    (*He stops crushing ice*)

Why you running that machine over me? Can't you see I'm trying to save this child's life!

ROSE

I can save myself.
(*Beat. Realizes she crossed an invisible line*)
I mean . . . I know what I'm doing. I got plans.

LAURA MAE

What kind of plans?

A beat. The only answer ROSE *can come up with is . . .*

ROSE

This ain't gonna be a forever thing.

Beat.

LAURA MAE

Never should have dropped out of college. Shame. Ain't even complete one semester.

ROSE

It wasn't for me.

LAURA MAE

There're other schools beside Texas A&M. Should've gone / back—

ROSE

School wasn't for me.

LAURA MAE

Then why didn't you just join the military? That's why you went to
Texas A&M in the first place. Just gave up. Ain't done shit.

Beat.

ROSE

I moved my mama out the neighborhood. Y'all ain't the only ones
can leave the neighborhood.
    (Beat)
Daddy. My food ready?

DUBBA J

Naw. Not yet.

ROSE

Then forget it. I lost my appetite.

DUBBA J

You got me making all this food.

ROSE

I'll get it in the morning.

DUBBA J

ROSIE!

ROSE

I got business. Gotta pick up money some dude owe Kingston.
Messing 'round here got me late. Time is money.

(She goes to the sliding glass door and peeps out the blinds)

Damn! They ain't left yet.

DUBBA J

The news station?

ROSE

The police. Damn. How am I gonna get over . . .

(A look of horror spreads across her face)

SHIT! Daddy. I hate to ask but I need a really big favor. I just need a place / to stash—

LAURA MAE

You got your people mixed up / if you—

ROSE

Daddy!

LAURA MAE

Why you got shit on you and you know the police / out here—

ROSE

I forgot. Shit!

LAURA MAE

What you need our help for? I thought you can save yourself.

ROSE

Awwwwwwwwww, c'mon. I ain't got time for this. How 'bout this? Mama, name your price.

LAURA MAE

What price?

ROSE

How much I need to pay you to stash my stuff?

LAURA MAE

You get your ass out of here. I ain't got time for games.

ROSE

I ain't playing games. Name your price. Square business.

ROSE *pulls a fat roll of bills out of her bra.*

LAURA MAE

We don't want your blood money. Ain't that right Dubba J?
   (DUBBA J *stares at the dough*)
Dubba J!

ROSE

I ain't ask daddy. I ask you. Name it and it's yours. Square business.

DUBBA J

Laura Mae, she waiting.

LAURA MAE

Her ass can keep on waiting till Gabriel come down from heaven and blow his horn.

DUBBA J

Now, Laura Mae, let's just think this through.

LAURA MAE	DUBBA J
Have you lost your goddamn / mind?	I just say one thing and your / ass blow up—

LAURA MAE	DUBBA J
What the hell you gotta think / through—	We supposed to be on / one accord—

ROSE

I ain't got all night.

JON-JON

Two hundred dollars!

ROSE

Sounds like a fair deal to me.

(She pulls the drugs out of her sock and puts the dope and the money on the counter)

Guard this with your life. I'll be back in twenty, thirty minutes.

(She runs to the door)

And don't just stand there. Hide it.

ROSE *leaves.* JON-JON *locks up.* DUBBA J *takes the money, leaving the drugs exposed. Four pistachio-size blue baggies of crack. They stare at it—afraid to move closer.*

LAURA MAE

So that's what it looks like. Looks like li'l pebbles.

JON-JON

That's why they call it rock.

DUBBA J

Wonder how they use it?

JON-JON

Oh. You put it in a glass pipe with that orange wirey stuff in the kitchen. Then you heat it up and puff with a cigarette lighter. You smoke it. Like this.

(He demonstrates. LAURA MAE *gives* JON-JON *a look)*

What? I saw it on *Nightline* with Ted Koppel.

A police siren in the distance. Everyone freezes.

LAURA MAE

Hide it!

DUBBA J *takes the drugs and runs behind the showcase counter. Then the siren fades away.*

JON-JON

No. No. You shouldn't hide it back there. Because we're the only ones that really go back there. You need to put it someplace that anybody who comes into the candy house could hide it. You should put it . . . hmmmmmmmmmmm . . . Let me see . . . Put it behind the boxes underneath the snow cone table. In that corner by the door where people stand.

(DUBBA J *takes the crack and hides it per his son's directions*)

Because somebody could come in and act like they're tying their shoes and just hide it there and we would never know. Therefore, we can claim innocence.

DUBBA J

Well look at my boy. That's my boy.

LAURA MAE

It's time for you to take your little wannabe-grown ass home, for sho. Come on!

JON-JON

What did I do?

LAURA MAE

What you know about smoking and hiding drugs? Ought to be shame of yourself. And I don't care what you saw on *Nightline*. That shit ain't cute.

JON-JON

Daddy, can I have my sip of beer before I go?

LAURA MAE

Jon-Jon!

JON-JON

Mama please. It's been a long night.

DUBBA J *goes to the fridge, grabs a beer, and pours some in a red cup.*

LAURA MAE

Dubba J, don't you dare. Not in front of me.

DUBBA J

Then don't look, shit. This boy earned his sippy-sip!

JON-JON

That's right. I earned it.

(DUBBA J *pours a li'l bit of beer in his son's cup.*)

Just a li'l teeny bit more . . .

(DUBBA J *gives him a bit more*)

Okay just a li'l bit more than that.

DUBBA J *pours some more.*

LAURA MAE

STOP! Dubba J. He's twelve years old!

JON-JON

What do we toast to, daddy?

DUBBA J

To Manhood.

DUBBA J and JON-JON

TO MANHOOD!

They toast. Bottoms up.
End of Scene.

ACT ONE – SCENE TWO

The next day. Noontime.

ROSE *fixes herself a Frito pie. Normally* DUBBA J *would do this, but he's dozed off in the TV chair. He snores.*

The jalapeños jar got a pitiful few peppers floating in the juice.

ROSE

Daddy, I know you ain't out of jalapeños.
(She looks under the table. Nada)
Awwwwwww hell. This don't make no damn sense. Daddy!
Daddy!
(Sees he's asleep. She goes over and kicks his foot)
WAKE YOUR ASS UP.
(He wakes up)
If you that damn sleepy you need to carry your ass to the house.

DUBBA J

You watch how you talk to me. Shit. Stayed up waiting on your ass all night.

ROSE

And I said I was sorry. Shit got hot. I couldn't go nowhere.
(Beat)
See. All cranky and shit. You had a really long night. Go home. If I was you I'd take a couple of days off.

54

                              DUBBA J

You trying to tell me how to run my business?

                               ROSE

No. I'm trying to tell you to take your ass home. After I finish
eating my Frito pie.

     (Beat)

Four sorry-ass peppers. What the hell am I supposed to do with
this?

     But that don't stop her from eating.

                              DUBBA J

You just watch. I'm gonna fix your ass. I'm gonna have a talk with
Kingston. Your ass ain't gonna be sitting up in here no more.

                               ROSE

Kingston the one that sent me. He been acting real strange lately.
Like he real worried 'bout you. Like for your safety and shit. Somebody fuck with you? You can tell me.

                              DUBBA J

Ain't nothing to tell. I don't know what put that in his head.

                               ROSE

Alright. We just looking out for you. That's what we supposed to
do. Look out for daddy. Anything wrong with that?

     (DUBBA J *doesn't answer*)

Anyway . . .

(ROSE goes to the kitchen to get some hot sauce. She pours it on her Frito pie)

Hey, daddy, you think mama's friend can hook me up? 'Cause I saw some Filas at Redbird Mall. Matches a red tracksuit I already got.

(A young woman, NICOLE, comes to the sliding glass door. She wears nursing scrubs. She sees ROSE. She hesitates to go inside)

She see me good and well. Watch her act like she don't see me and try and turn around and leave. Watch.

(NICOLE turns her back to the sliding glass door. She stands paralyzed on the patio. Not sure what to do)

See. Look. I told you. Nicole. Nicole! NICKY!
Now she gonna act like she don't hear me.

(ROSE goes to the sliding glass door and opens it)

Nicky? You coming to the candy house or not? Come on in. Daddy need some customers bad.

(NICOLE comes inside)

So how you?

NICOLE

Fine. You?

(ROSE doesn't answer. She just gives side-eye for that curt reply)

Paw-Paw. I come to pay my tab.

DUBBA J

You're late.

NICOLE

I know I'm late. I would have paid you on time but I been at my sister's house cause we ain't have no hot water in my unit. And I can't do cold showers. And I can't have me and my baby walking around funky. Especially in this heat. Plus my car in the shop. Ain't got no wheels. This been a rough month. But I'm here to settle my debt.

(She pulls out her coin purse)

Now here's my list and I tallied everything up for last month. I got a box of Boston Baked Beans. Two Watermelon Now and Laters. Four Cherry Now-Laters . . . Two Lime Now-Laters. Two Grape Now-Laters. Two Twix. Three boxes of Red Hots. Four Chick-O-Sticks. Two boxes of Lemonheads. Two pink and purple Nerds. Four orange, red, and green Nerds. Eight 7UPS. Three bags of Hot Fries. Four sour pickles. Three bags of pickle juice. One big bag of ice. Four cherry popsicles with the cream inside. Six snow cones. Five nachos. An extra thing of jalepeños. Four Frito pies. Two link sand-wiches. And a big bag of Jolly Ranchers. Plus a little extra for being late and an extra ten for watching Tamera them few days.

She pays.

DUBBA J

I suppose you want to start on your new tab?

NICOLE *looks at* ROSE.

NICOLE

Not today. I'll wait till Tamera come back home.

ROSE

Where's baby girl?

Away.

NICOLE *starts to leave.*

ROSE

So . . . I hear you got a big promotion? Mama be bragging on you. I heard it's something big.

NICOLE

I'm an L.V.N.

ROSE

What that stand for?

NICOLE

Licensed vocational nurse.

ROSE

Awwwww look at you. I hear you at Parkland now. Moving on up. I'm working on a promotion too.

(No reply from NICOLE*)*

We don't talk no more. I was just trying to catch up.

NICOLE

I have to finish getting ready for work. I don't have time to talk. Just came to pay my tab. Paw-Paw, we settled up?

DUBBA J

To the penny.

NICOLE

Good. Tell Mama Laura I said hi.

ROSE

You want me to walk with you back to your place?

NICOLE

What?

ROSE

You shouldn't be out walking by yourself. Not after what happened last night.

NICOLE

What happened last night?

ROSE

You don't know?

DUBBA J

Somebody shot a li'l girl yesterday. A damn shame.

NICOLE

Where? Here?

ROSE

Over by the swimming pool. Last night. Got crime scene tape everywhere.

DUBBA J

How you don't know? It was all on the news!

NICOLE

My sister real holiness. She don't believe in television.

ROSE

Shantay holiness? Shiiiiit, you for real? She used to be all out there. Shoot, the three of us used to get into all kinds of trouble. The three amigos.

NICOLE

Some of us see the error of our ways and choose to get our shit together.

A beat.

ROSE *'s beeper goes off.*

ROSE

Saved by the bell . . . or . . . the . . . beeper.
   (She checks the number)
Daddy, check ya later.
   (She starts to leave, then stops)
Look. I'm just asking you this as a friend. Square business. Where's Tamera?

NICOLE

At my sister's.

ROSE

Good. You might want to keep her there 'til shit blow over.

ROSE *strolls out.*

A look washes over NICOLE*'s face.*

DUBBA J

You okay?

NICOLE

I need to sit down.

(She sits in a folding chair)

I told you something like this might happen.

DUBBA J

I ain't signing that damn petition.

NICOLE

Paw-Paw!

DUBBA J

What the hell is a petition supposed to do anyway?

NICOLE

Make somebody do the right thing. Shame them. Threaten them. Sue them. Whatever it takes. Make them do the right thing. Evict Kingston. It's that simple.

DUBBA J

It's never that simple.

NICOLE

It is that simple. The rent office is just looking the other way. They're taking rent money from a known drug dealer. They're

61

letting him operate a crack house out of these apartments. Our neighborhood. That's blood money. And if we don't speak up that shit's just gonna keep happening. Paw-Paw, the petition is just the beginning. We got a whole plan laid out. But we gotta start somewhere. And we can't wait for somebody else's baby to get shot.

DUBBA J

How many signatures you got?

NICOLE

Four.
But if you sign the petition I can get more signatures. People trust you. People respect you. And they'll be less afraid to sign if they know you signed. Paw-Paw!

DUBBA J

You could get yourself in a world of trouble.

NICOLE

So we just stand by and do nothing?

The front door flies open. JON-JON *runs inside, rushing behind the counter.*

JON-JON

Hi, daddy. Hi, Nicky.

DUBBA J

Boy, you left the door wide open.

JON-JON

Mama right behind me.

(JON-JON *puts his left hand on the cashbox and holds his right hand in the air, à la Jimmy Stewart in* It's A Wonderful Life)

I wish I had a million dollars. Hot dog!

JON-JON *grabs an apron. It is just like his dad's. It reads "Paw-Paw's Candy Tree."* LAURA MAE *comes in. She wears nursing scrubs and carries a bag of food.*

LAURA MAE

Girl, Nicole, I am glad to see you. Been thinking about you all night long. Where that petition? I wanna sign. Jon-Jon signing, too.

DUBBA J

Laura Mae!

LAURA MAE

Your ass gonna sign too, Dubba J.

NICOLE

I got it at the house.

LAURA MAE

Well what you waiting on! Go get it!

NICOLE

Well I actually I got two petitions: one for city hall and one for the county commissioner.

I will sign anything you put in my face if it gets that trash up outta our neighborhood.

DUBBA J

Awwwwww shit!

LAURA MAE

You just go ahead and eat that goddamn Grandy's I brought you. Leave me alone. And Nicky baby, I wasn't planning on coming up here this weekend. But for you, I'm gonna be here first thing Saturday morning. And I will make every man, woman, and child that come through that door sign your petition.

NICOLE

Both of 'em?

LAURA MAE

(Raising her hand in the air)
Every last one. Here my hand to God.
And I'll make Kingston's boys sign them petitions. And Rosie, too. Watch me. Girl! Go get those petitions!
NICOLE *gives* LAURA MAE *a big kiss on the cheek.*

NICOLE

I love you, Mama Laura!

LAURA MAE

You know I'd do anything for you, baby girl.
(NICOLE *gushes as she races out)*

Dubba J, you signing them goddamn petitions. I ain't letting your ass off the hook. Not this time.

(DUBBA J *mumbles something under his breath*)

Mumble all you want. I don't care.

And you know I'm gonna tell you all 'bout yourself. Had me worried all night long. You not coming home.

DUBBA J

Every time you called I told you I was okay.

LAURA MAE

That wasn't good enough. I had to lay eyes on you myself. What kind of wife would I be if I just took your word for it?

(To JON-JON*)*

And take off that apron. You know you not staying. You coming to the nursing home with me. Watch Shirley Temple movies with the old white people where it's safe.

ROSE *comes back in through the sliding glass door.*

ROSE

Is that Grandy's? I want some Grandy's.

LAURA MAE

Don't you have somewhere to be?

ROSE

Awwwwww, Mama. I don't get no proper greeting?

LAURA MAE *turns on the TV. She turns it to a channel showing a commercial for carpet cleaning.*

LAURA MAE

Do proper. You get proper.

(*To herself*)

Let's see what Channel 8 got to say.

ROSE

About the shooting? All they do is a bunch of overexaggerating.

LAURA MAE

Overexaggerating? The truth is the truth. If that make you feel guilty then that's your problem.

(*An anchor appears on screen with the words* FEAR AND OUTRAGE IN PLEASANT GROVE)

Look! Fear and Outrage in Pleasant Grove! Here we go.

ROSE

See. Fear and outrage! That's all for ratings. Like how they always find the craziest-looking Black woman—

JON-JON

Mama look! You on TV!

IT SURE IS LAURA MAE! *She's dressed same as the night before.* JON-JON *turns up the volume.*

LAURA MAE ON TV

Why Lord! Lord! Whyyyyyyyyy! THEY SHOOTING THE BABIES! NOT THE BABIES. LORD!!!!!!!!!!!!!!

THE REPORTER

Ma'am, can you tell us / who—

LAURA MAE ON TV

Get that BLEEP camera out my face! MOVE! JON-JON! MAMA
COMING!!!! JON-JOOOOOOOOOOOOOOOOOOOOOOON!!!!!

*LAURA MAE hurries to turn the TV off. Then falls back into her chair.
Devastated! She starts to cry.*

The phone rings.

JON-JON

That's probably somebody from church.

LAURA MAE cries louder. ROSE stops the phone from ringing.

DUBBA J

Awwwww, Cookie. Baby, it's gonna be okay.

LAURA MAE

I'm so embarrassed. That hurt my feelings. Why they gotta show
me like that? I was just scared.

Everybody goes to comfort her.

JON-JON

Mama, don't cry.

ROSE

I know what will make you happy. Daddy got a surprise for you.

What kind of surprise?

ROSE

Something you been wishing for.

DUBBA J

Rosie!

LAURA MAE

It's not what I think it is?

ROSE

It might be. Daddy got it hidden in the bedroom closet. Go see.

LAURA MAE *goes into the bedroom.*

DUBBA J

That supposed to be for her birthday.

ROSE

I was just trying to cheer her up.

NICOLE *comes to the sliding glass door with the petitions. She sees* ROSE *and leaves. They don't see her.*

LAURA MAE

(Yelling from the bedroom)
Ha! That's what I'm talking 'bout.
(She comes out with a badass red suit-dress. She holds it against her body and struts)

Look at me. Look at me. That's what I'm talking 'bout. Cold-blooded, knock-'em-dead red. HA! I can't wait for Sunday morning. I'm gonna be the baddest thang up in Lord's Missionary. And when that no-good Sister Mae-Helen lay her eyes on me. Baby, this outfit gonna shut her ass up real good.

ROSE

Now don't that make you feel better?

LAURA MAE

Dubba J, how you know this the outfit I wanted? Look at you paying attention and shit.

DUBBA J

And that ain't all. I got you a new hat, them shoes you had your eyes on. Shit, I even got you a fancy pair of stockings, too. But I'm saving that for your birthday.

ROSE

Daddy got it all stashed in a box under the sofa in the bedroom.

DUBBA J

Rosie!

LAURA MAE *twirls around. Sashaying and such.*

ROSE

Oooooh, mama. That dress bringing back memories. Baby, your fashion shows at the candy house! Your friends used to hook us up right. They gave us some good deals. Peaches was the one I remember most.

(Beat)

That man had some pretty toenails.

(LAURA MAE *still twirling and sashaying*)

Ooooooh, mama, look at you!

ROSE *joins in.* JON-JON *grabs a candy bar for a mic.*

JON-JON

(His best attempt at a French accent)

And now ladies and gentlemen, what the well-dressed drug dealer in 1988 will be wearing. Straight from the exotic locales of Taiwan. The House of FILA.

ROSE *is giving her best church fashion show strutting and posing. Cheers and applause from all.*

LAURA MAE

Those were the good ole days. Used to have some nice times, didn't we? I used to say Peaches coming through on Friday, y'all. Baby, Friday roll around, the candy house be packed. Ladies walk in dressed like Florida Evans. Walk out looking like Dominique Deveraux.

ROSE

I miss those days.

JON-JON

Mama, the security tag still on the dress. See.

LAURA MAE

Awwwwww hell! That's the third time Denise done this shit.

People just don't take pride in their work no more. Dubba J, didn't you notice the tag?

JON-JON

Maybe that's God's way of telling you that you shouldn't buy stolen clothes.

LAURA MAE

You need to watch that smart mouth. Talking smart to your mama. I don't know what done got into you. Too many bad influences.

JON-JON

Like the kind that shoplift clothes?

LAURA MAE

Keep it up. Keep it up. But I'm about to have the last laugh. 'Cause mama got plans for you.

JON-JON

What kind of plans?

LAURA MAE

Remember last summer?

JON-JON *gasps in horror.*

DUBBA J

You wouldn't dare.

LAURA MAE

I done already put in the phone call.

No!!!

LAURA MAE

I'm signing your ass up for Vacation Bible School.

JON-JON *runs to* DUBBA J *for help.*

JON-JON

Daddy! Daddy, please. I don't wanna go to Vacation Bible School. ANYTHING but Vacation Bible School. Please don't let her do this.

LAURA MAE

Candy Man can't help you now. I'm running this shit.

DUBBA J

Laura Mae, I never thought I'd see you stoop so low.

LAURA MAE

And I want you to get kicked out this time. Try it. Try it. Getting kicked out of Vacation Bible School on the first goddamn day. I've never been so embarrassed.

ROSE

It ain't that white church from Seagoville that be parked on Pemberton Hill in that ugly *Partridge Family*-looking bus, with the lady that got the *Brady Bunch* mama hair who be handing out Bibles and *700 Club* refrigerator magnets?

LAURA MAE

That's the one.

ROSE

Awwwwww hell. Those white folks don't mess around. They
snatched up one of my best workers. I tried to lure Dante off the
bus. He started speaking in tongues.

LAURA MAE

Hear that Jon-Jon? You gonna be speaking in tongues. Yes sir,
'cause I'm gonna get some Jesus in your little narrow black ass if
it's the last muthafucking thing I do.

JON-JON

(Crying)
I need beer.

LAURA MAE

See that's your damn problem right there.

*There is a loud banging at the front door. Then more pounding. And
silence.*

DUBBA J

Who the fuck is that?

More pounding.

ROSE

Five-oh. Fuck. Five-oh. They back. Daddy, lock the door. Lock the
door. Shit. It's the police. Five-oh.

DUBBA J *pulls the blinds and locks up.*

LAURA MAE *and son run and hide in the bedroom. Now there is banging at the sliding glass door.* ROSE *runs and hides in the bathroom.* DUBBA J *ducks behind the candy counter.*

The bedroom door cracks open. LAURA MAE *looks out.*

DONNIE
(Yelling through the sliding glass door—unseen)
Open this goddamn door. Dubba J! Open this goddamn door. Dubba J!

DUBBA J
Donnie!

LAURA MAE *comes out.* JON-JON *follows.*

DONNIE
(Unseen)
Open this muthafucking door. Or I'm calling the police.

More banging on the sliding glass door.

LAURA MAE
What the hell is his goddamn problem banging on our / door like—

LAURA MAE *rushes to the door. But* DUBBA J *beats her to it.*

DUBBA J
Laura Mae! Laura Mae! Let me handle it!

(More banging)
Step back now. I'm handling this.

DONNIE

Open this goddamn door, Dubba J.

DUBBA J

Now, Donnie, I don't know what your problem is. But you need to calm the fuck down.

Now there's banging at the front door again.

DONNIE

I'm getting in this muthafucka. One way or the other.
Now there's kicking at the front door.

DUBBA J

This fool done lost his damn mind.

LAURA MAE *opens the door.* DONNIE *storms in carrying a baseball bat.*

DONNIE

Where he at? Where his ass at?

LAURA MAE

Where who at?

DUBBA J

Donnie, calm down. Just calm the fuck down.

DONNIE

DON JR.! WHERE YOUR ASS AT BOY?

DUBBA J

Your boy ain't here.

DONNIE *shoves* DUBBA J *out the way and searches the apartment. He sees the bedroom is empty. But the bathroom door is locked.*

DONNIE

Why this door locked? He's in there. You're hiding him.

DONNIE *kicks the bathroom door.*

DUBBA J

Oh shit!

DONNIE

Open this goddamn door. Boy, don't make me break it down.

LAURA MAE *and* JON-JON *run into the kitchen.*

DUBBA J

Donnie! Stop man! C'mon, brother.

DUBBA J *takes hold of* DONNIE *and tries to calm his friend.*

DONNIE

You let me go. That's my son.

DUBBA J

C'mon, brother. Be cool. Be cool.

DONNIE

You a goddamn lie. I know he here.

(DUBBA J *tussles with* DONNIE *trying to get him to drop the bat*)

Let me go! Let me go!

DUBBA J

Now you making a goddamn fool of yourself. Don Jr. ain't here. I told you. Your boy not here.

DONNIE

Bullshit!

Out of frustration DONNIE *swings the bat and knocks over a tower of snow cone cups.*

DUBBA J

Awwwwwww hell naw. That's my shit.

LAURA MAE *grabs the cordless phone off the TV table and runs to the kitchen.* DONNIE *keeps* DUBBA J *away with the bat.*

DONNIE

Man, get away from me. I just want my son. That's all I want.

DUBBA J

Brother, come on.

I said get back.

> DUBBA J *takes another step.* DONNIE *takes a swing at* DUBBA J, *but misses.*

JON-JON

Daddy!!!!!

DUBBA J

Awwwwwww. You done fucked up now!

> DUBBA J *gets ready to charge.*

> LAURA MAE *comes out of the kitchen with the cordless phone.*

LAURA MAE

DONNIE! PUT THAT GODDAMN BAT DOWN! Or I'm calling your wife!
(DONNIE *drops the bat.* DUBBA J *picks it up*)
Jon-Jon. Get Miss Juanita on the phone.

> JON-JON *takes the phone and goes to the kitchen.*

DONNIE

You said / you wouldn't—

LAURA MAE

I lied.

DUBBA J

Sit your crazy ass in that goddamn chair and calm the fuck down.

*(*DONNIE *takes a seat)*

What the hell done got into you?

> DONNIE

I'm looking for my boy.

> LAURA MAE

What happened to Don Jr.?

> DONNIE

He hasn't been home since Sunday night.

> *Alarmed,* LAURA MAE *goes to the kitchen to take the phone from* JON-JON. *He's been trying to get through with no luck. She dials.*

> DUBBA J

What's that got to do with you breaking up my place?

> DONNIE

Somebody said they just saw him at the candy house.

> DUBBA J

Somebody lied to your ass.

*(*DONNIE *starts to huff like he's having trouble breathing)*

Your muthafucking ass got the asthma and shit and you running around here acting a goddamn fool. Jon-Jon, get this man some ice water. Shit.

> JON-JON *does as he is told.*

I keep getting a busy signal.

Why we just finding out the baby missing? We're supposed to be friends.

                    DONNIE

Some friends.

                    DUBBA J

What the hell you mean by that?

                    DONNIE

What you think I mean?

    JON-JON *comes out with the water and gives it to* DONNIE.

                    JON-JON

Here you go, Mr. Donnie.

    (Beat)

I saw Don Jr. yesterday.

                    DONNIE

When?

                    JON-JON

When the shooting happened. He was in here with some of them boys that stand on the corner. They were all here buying candy and then some boy ran in and said the girl got shot. Then they all ran out.

    A noise comes from the bathroom.

DONNIE

Who in that bathroom?

DUBBA J

Nobody in that bathroom!

DONNIE *gets up and heads for the bathroom. He grabs the bat from* DUBBA J.

DONNIE

Who in this bathroom? Who in here?

DUBBA J *rushes over to try and stop* DONNIE.

DUBBA J

DONNIE! STOP IT!

DONNIE *shoves* DUBBA J *away.*

DONNIE

Open this muthafucking door.

DONNIE *kicks the bathroom door open.* ROSE *comes out. She yanks the bat out of* DONNIE*'s hand and throws it to the ground. She shoves him back with great force.*

ROSE

Dude, you got a fucking problem or what?

(DONNIE *storms back over. 'Bout to be some shit)*

Oh. Oh. Okay!

ROSE *meets* DONNIE. DUBBA J *jumps between them.*

DUBBA J

He don't mean no trouble. He just looking for his boy.

ROSE

Is your boy the skinny kid with the braces on his teeth?

DONNIE

That's him. You know where he is?

ROSE

No. But he'll turn up. He sticks out like a sore thumb.
    (She chuckles)
I've never met a drug dealer with braces.

DONNIE

Ain't shit funny.

ROSE

You know what's not funny? The one hundred dollars' worth of
product I flushed down the toilet 'cause I thought you were the
police. You owe me.

DONNIE

I'm not giving you a goddamn thing.

ROSE

Come again?

DONNIE

You lowlife piece of muthafucking trash.

ROSE

What you call me?

DONNIE

I called you a lowlife piece of shit.

ROSE *hits* DONNIE *in the nose with the butt of her gun. Blood flies.* DONNIE *falls to the ground.* LAURA MAE *grabs* JON-JON *and quickly pulls him close to protect her child.*

LAURA MAE

Oh my God.

ROSE

I'm a CAPITALIST, muthafucka.

Let's try it again. Where my hundred dollars?

DONNIE

I don't have a hundred dollars.

ROSE

You better get it from somewhere.

DUBBA J

ROSE!

(He takes money out the cash box and gives it to her. ROSE *looks around at the family, as if she's coming out of a daze, or coming off autopilot)*

Now leave him alone!!

ROSE

He called me out my name.

ROSE *storms out.* LAURA MAE *grabs a wet towel from the kitchen to help* DONNIE.

DONNIE

You can't wipe your guilt away with blood money. It don't work that way.

DUBBA J

What guilt?

DONNIE

Don't play stupid. Everybody knows.

LAURA MAE

Donnie, stop talking. Your nose bleeding. You're making a mess. I'm trying to help your ass.

She somehow gets DONNIE *settled enough to help him clean his nose. A brief, quiet moment of calm, then something catches* DONNIE*'s attention.*

DONNIE

Is that my TV?
(*Points to the TV*)
That's my television.

DUBBA J

Alright. Hold up now.

DONNIE

Hold up, my ass. That's my goddamn television. Some lowlife stole my TV and you muthafuckas / bought our shit.

DUBBA J

This our TV right here.

DONNIE

Slap that muthafucka on the left side it come on. Don't it!?!

(DONNIE *goes to see.* DUBBA J *blocks him*)

What you trying to hide?

LAURA MAE

Donnie! Donnie!

DONNIE *backs off.*

DONNIE

Fuck it! You want the goddamn TV so bad, you can have it. But you can't have my son.

(Beat)

Couldn't you have told your friends to stay away from our boy? That he off-limits like Jon-Jon off-limits.

DUBBA J

They're not my friends. I ain't got nothing / to do—

DONNIE

That's a lie. Everybody know this place ain't nothing but a front.

DUBBA J

Donnie . . . brother . . . This ain't no front. I promise you, brother.

DONNIE

Call me brother one more time.

DUBBA J

I can't call you brother?

DONNIE

You're not my brother. My brother wouldn't do the shit you've done. Jon-Jon say he saw my boy running with them dope dealers. If Jon-Jon saw him then you saw him, too. Couldn't you have stepped in for my boy? Snatch him up. My brother would look after my son. You're not my brother.

DONNIE *starts for the door to leave.*

LAURA MAE

Donnie . . . Can you ask Juanita to call me? Please.

DONNIE

Juanita don't want to talk to you. We don't want shit to do with you.

DONNIE *leaves. A long silence.*

LAURA MAE

Dubba J, I want out! I want you to shut this place down.

86

DUBBA J

Laura Mae! Baby just calm / down.

LAURA MAE

The man I married would have snatched that boy up just like
Donnie said. What? You afraid of Kingston?

DUBBA J

I ain't afraid of no muthafucka.

A beat. LAURA MAE *wants to say she doesn't believe him. But it hurts
to admit that.*

LAURA MAE

The candy house is over. At least it is for me—And Jon-Jon.

LAURA MAE *and* JON-JON *leave.*
DUBBA J *goes back to his TV chair and slumps into it. He slams his
hands on the TV table out of frustration and the TV comes on. A
commercial for Grandy's plays—an old white woman hawking
chicken-fried steak and cream gravy for $2.99.*

End of Scene.

ACT ONE – SCENE THREE

Same day—nighttime.

DUBBA J *counts up what little money is in the cashbox. Not much. Just a few bills. Some ones. Maybe a five or two.*
He goes out the sliding glass door and steps out on the patio. He looks around. Nothing. Quiet. Inside, there is a loud thud against the candy table wall. That gets his attention. Another loud thud. He goes back inside, leaving the sliding glass door open.

Another thud—then screaming from next door. A man screaming bloody murder. Screaming and crying like a child.
And then there's quiet.

But after a very brief spell of quiet . . . then two more thuds. DUBBA J *sees the open sliding glass door. He rushes and closes it. Then he grabs his keys and the money box, and makes ready to leave.*

There's a knock at the sliding glass door. DUBBA J *doesn't answer. Another knock.*

NICOLE

(Unseen)
Paw-Paw, it's me. Open up! Please!

DUBBA J *hurries and lets* NICOLE *in. She wears a T-shirt that says "Re-Elect Ragsdale in 87."*

DUBBA J

You alright?

NICOLE

She died.

DUBBA J

What?

NICOLE

The little girl. She died a few minutes ago.

DUBBA J

But she was just shot in the leg.

NICOLE

The bullet caused a blood clot that killed her.
    (Beat)
Playing at a swimming pool with her friends. Now she's dead.

DUBBA J

My God.

NICOLE *reaches into her pocket and pulls out a pen and some folded sheets of paper.*

NICOLE

No more time for half-stepping. Remember this morning, I only had four signatures. I got twenty-eight now.

DUBBA J

That's still not a lot.

NICOLE

But that's twenty-four more than what I had. And they came to me.
I didn't have to go to them. That proves to me I'm doing the right
thing.

DUBBA J

I'm worried about you.

NICOLE

Too late for that. We called an emergency meeting of the Neighborhood Crime Watch for tomorrow morning. And I promised that
I will have your signature. And that you'll let us have the crime
watch meeting at the candy house.

DUBBA J

You done lost your damn mind!

NICOLE

A little girl was murdered in our neighborhood. And what do we do
about it?

DUBBA J

You call the police.

NICOLE

Miss Etta Collins called the police. They shot her dead. She was
seventy years old. Mr. David Horton, he was eighty-one years old.

He called the police and the police shot him dead outside the senior citizen home he lived at. Seems like black folks call the police and they get shot . . . by the police. So what you propose we do?

DUBBA J

Nicole, you going 'bout this the wrong way. If you don't feel safe, find some different way to solve the problem. Find someplace better. What about where your sister lives? Is it safe there?

NICOLE

I ain't running like a fugitive when I ain't done shit wrong.

DUBBA J

Then fine. Stay. But don't be stupid.

NICOLE

Stupid is not speaking up. That's what stupid is.

DUBBA J

You really think Kingston gonna be scared over a goddamn petition?

NICOLE

No. But the rent office will be. Evict Kingston. That's all I'm asking. And if they don't, we got folks in high places gonna come down on their ass.

DUBBA J

Nicky, use your head. Shit, you already said you don't trust the police. So you run off Kingston, then what you got? You need to think twice 'bout who you trying to run up outta here.

(Beat)

Be smart. Think shit through. Those same boys on the corner was causing trouble long before Kingston got here. Right 'fore school started back. 'Fore we even ever heard the name Kingston. And they wasn't just on the corner. They was all around here fucking with folks. I don't know how it all happened. Didn't see it coming. Shit, one day we look around and them boys had lost they goddamn mind. But Kingston got here, cleaned all that shit up. You forget? Go ask Miss Tossie. She remember. One of them boys gave her a black eye. Sixteen-year-old boy attacking a woman old enough to be his great-granny. She come up in the candy house looking pitiful with that black eye and Kingston was here. He made her tell him what happened. Then he walked with her to the corner. Found the boy that hit her and he beat that muthafucka bloody. Then made him get on his knees and apologize to Miss Tossie and give her all the money in his pocket. Made all his partners on the corner give Miss Tossie every dollar they had too. Down to the last goddamn penny. Never had no more trouble out them boys. Kingston did that.

A sizeable beat. NICOLE *considers.*

NICOLE

We can add you to the petition, too.

DUBBA J

Say what?
Ain't you listen to a goddamn word I said?

NICOLE

I heard you loud and clear. If you're not with us then you're against us. Paw-Paw, sign the petitions. Show us where you stand. Or we will demand they evict you right along with Kingston. The candy house a threat to the neighborhood.

DUBBA J

What the fuck you say?

NICOLE	DUBBA J
The candy house no better than the crack / house.	Whoa! Whoa! Whoa!

NICOLE

Sign this petition or we gonna put all your business on front street.

DUBBA J

I ain't got nothing to hide.

NICOLE

We'll find something if we dig hard enough. And if we don't, I'll make shit up if I have to.

DUBBA J

You would do that to me?

NICOLE

I don't want to. But I will if it comes to that.

DUBBA J

Me and Laura Mae been there for you when no one else was. Kept your fast ass out of juvie. Kept you outta all kinds of trouble. And after everything we done for you, you gonna turn around and shit on us like that? Oughta be ashamed of yourself.

NICOLE

You're afraid to sign the petition. Oughta be ashamed of yourself.

DUBBA J

Get the hell outta my place.

(NICOLE *storms off. But gets to the sliding glass door and stops. She starts to cry*)

You alright? Nicole? Nicky? Girl, stop crying them goddamn crocodile tears!

(NICOLE *turns around. She ain't shed nary a tear. She gives him a shitty look*)

See! You was crying crocodile tears. I knew it. You used to do that at the truancy courts in front of the judge. All that crying and shaking and carrying on. I'm the one that taught you that shit. You can't fool me.

NICOLE

Well goddammit, I gotta do something.

DUBBA J

You watch that language in front of me.

NICOLE

Paw-Paw. I'm counting on you. Please. We need your support. This is a good neighborhood. I don't want that to change. Do you?

DUBBA J

No.

NICOLE

Then you know what you have to do.

DUBBA J

You running around here talking 'bout safety and shit. But then
you waving that goddamn petition around, don't you see that could
put your baby in more danger?

NICOLE

Well I think being friends with Kingston and his crew puts your son
in danger.
   (Beat)
At work, a nurse on my shift told me a story about these two kids.
Teenagers that worked for the Jamaicans. Somebody tricked them
into thinking the police were going to bust them. So they flushed
all their drugs down the toilet. When the Jamaicans came and the
kids didn't have the money or the drugs, they stripped them naked.
Slashed their backs with razor blades. Poured salt in the wounds
and then poured scalding hot water on their backs. They shot one
in the head but let the other live to be a walking reminder to friend
and foe, not to cross them. That's the kind of person you're letting
around your son.

DUBBA J

Kingston's not like . . .

NICOLE

They're all like that. And Kingston is no different.

A beat. Maybe she has him . . . but then . . . a knock at the sliding glass door.

KINGSTON

Pupa. It's me.

DUBBA J

(Under his breath)
Now is not the goddamn time. GO!

KINGSTON

Pupa!

DUBBA J

Now!

*She hurries to the bedroom to hide. But she's left the petitions on the candy counter. She tries to retrieve them but is too late—*DUBBA J *is opening the sliding glass door before she can get to the counter. She runs back to the bedroom.*

KINGSTON *comes in holding a dishrag.*

KINGSTON

Pupa. I have something for you. Close your eyes, I got a good surprise.
   *(*DUBBA J *doesn't)*
I said close your eyes.
   *(*DUBBA J *closes his eyes.* KINGSTON *puts the dishrag in* DUBBA J *'s hands)*
Now open your eyes.

                          DUBBA J

What is it?

                          KINGSTON

Open it.

> DUBBA J *goes to the candy counter. Quickly dumping it on top the*
> *petitions to hide them from* KINGSTON.

                          DUBBA J

Tell me what it is first.

                          KINGSTON

Pupa, come on! Open it.

> DUBBA J *opens the rag to reveal a bloody severed hand, four fingers,*
> *sliced mid-palm. One of the fingers has a ring on it.* DUBBA J *jumps*
> *back.*

                          DUBBA J

GODDAMN!

                          KINGSTON

Pupa, I found the piece of shit that stole your wedding ring. Take
that cheap piece of shit off.

(DUBBA J *does.* KINGSTON *examines it)*

Almost a perfect match. Mommy never noticed. Did she? I did
good. Didn't I?
Stealing from the Candy Man. A nice old man. Never hurt nobody.
Bastard get what he deserve.

DUBBA J

You didn't have to go chop off his hand.

KINGSTON

He threaten you?

(DUBBA J *nods yes*)

He scare you? Then he get no pity from me. Awww pupa, don't look that way.

DUBBA J

Boy, have you lost your goddamn mind? The police was just in here. Eyeballin' my place. Now you coming with a muthafucking hand.

KINGSTON

What police was it?

DUBBA J

It was a Black cop and a white cop. That's all I know.

KINGSTON

Was it the Black cop with the big, nasty, hairy-ass mole over his right eye?

DUBBA J

Yeah, that ugly muthafucka.

KINGSTON

You ain't gotta worry about them. Him and his partner, they're mi friends. So they're your friends, too. They look out for us. Now to the matter at hand.

(He chuckles at his joke as he begins to slice the finger with his hunting knife)

How he get this little ring on his fat-ass finger?

KINGSTON

DUBBA J

Hey! Hey! Hey! Don't do that shit in front of me.

KINGSTON goes to the kitchen. DUBBA J slyly grabs the petitions and dumps them in the trash can. KINGSTON starts to slice.

KINGSTON

Fuck. I'm gonna have to cut some more bone.

(He puts on a Paw-Paw's Candy Tree apron)

You know pupa, we need to talk about mommy. She was really ugly to me. Last night I tried to walk her to the car like I always do. She told me to fuck-off. But I always walk her to the car and try to do polite things. And she cuss me. I got feelings, pupa. I got feelings—Goddamn there's a lot of bone—Talk to mommy. 'Cause I don't deserve that. I try to be a good person. Almost done. Just one more . . . DONE!

(Then he takes one of DUBBA J's meat cleavers and hacks up the hand with great flourish, and puts the pieces in the garbage disposal and turns it on. KINGSTON comes out of the kitchen and puts the ring on the candy counter. DUBBA J reaches for it but KINGSTON covers it up)

Where is it?

DUBBA J

Where's what?

The papers that was here. The papers that you put the rag on to keep me from seeing what it was.

KINGSTON

DUBBA J

It was just some trash a customer left behind.

KINGSTON

Your name wouldn't happen to be on that—trash?

DUBBA J

I don't know what you mean.

KINGSTON

I'm not stupid. I saw her come in.

Your friend? The one who brought the papers you hiding. Where is she?

(DUBBA J *doesn't answer*)

Come out. Come out. Wherever you are. Who back here?

He moves toward the bedroom.

DUBBA J

BOY! You bring your ass over here!

(DUBBA J*'s gamble paid off.* KINGSTON *drops his head and goes to* DUBBA J *like a kid 'bout to be reprimanded by his dad. IT WORKED!* DUBBA J—*in a hushed -private tone.*)

Shit! Comin' up in here trying to cause trouble in my place. Son you know better than that. Now if you got a problem with anybody in the candy house, you let me handle it. Respect the candy house. You know I don't play that shit.

                    KINGSTON
I'm sorry. You right, pupa. I can always count on you to get mi head right.
    (Chuckles)
Look at mi getting all carried away. WHO BACK HERE?

        They laugh. NICOLE *comes out with a canister of Mace aimed at* KINGSTON.

DUBBA J	KINGSTON
GODDAMN!	Raasclaat!

                    NICOLE
Paw-Paw, get back. I'll spray you too if I have to.

    KINGSTON *carefully tries to approach.*

                    NICOLE
Get the fuck away from me.

                    KINGSTON
Pupa, talk some sense into your friend.

                    NICOLE
I can think for myself.

Really? 'Cause everything not as black-and-white as you want it to be. You think I'm the devil. Then better the devil you know. Because what will come after me is not anything nice. Don't you want a home where your little girl can run, and play and not be afraid? I want that too. Can't you see? We both want the same thing. But if you get rid of me, that dream is fucked.

NICOLE

I don't believe that.

KINGSTON

You don't have a choice. We have to learn to coexist. Otherwise we die.

KINGSTON *takes another step.*

NICOLE

Take one more step and I'll burn your fucking eyes out. I swear to God.

KINGSTON

They sprayed us with Mace when I was twelve to tough us up. You think I'm afraid of Mace?

He takes another step. Her body tenses.

A wah di bloodclaat dew yuh, Stakki skunt?

NICOLE

What you say to me?

KINGSTON

I say you burn me. I break your fucking arm off.

He steps closer. NICOLE *hesitates one beat too long.*
KINGSTON *knocks the Mace out of her hand. Then grabs her arm and twists it behind her back. She winces in pain.*

DUBBA J

If I give you what you want, you let her go?

NICOLE

Paw-Paw!

DUBBA J *grabs the petitions.*

KINGSTON

Tear it to bits.

*(*DUBBA J *hesitates)*

Do it now.

*(*DUBBA J *tears the petitions into three parts)*

You lucky I'm not the Shower Posse. You'd be dead by now.

He lets her go.

DUBBA J

Nicky . . .

*(*NICOLE *rushes out of the candy house)*

Kingston, don't go after her. Please don't hurt her.

103

KINGSTON

Don't have to. She's smart. She'll come around. Sooner or later.

(He puts the ring on the candy counter and starts to leave . . . but stops)

Pupa? Your name wasn't on those papers. Was it?

DUBBA J

No.

A beat.

KINGSTON

I want to believe you, pupa. I really do.

KINGSTON *leaves.*

DUBBA J *locks up, then goes back to the candy counter, almost hugging it with his body. He tries to get his head together. The phone rings. He answers.*

DUBBA J

Laura Mae . . .

He goes to the TV and turns it on. The words "MURDER IN PLEASANT GROVE" fill the screen. The picture of a sweet little African American girl in a cheerleading outfit comes next.

An angry sound like cannons explodes outside. DUBBA J *drops the phone.*

*Now on TV, a police officer is talking. Then more scenes from the
neighborhood flash across the screen.*

*There's more loud banging and booming outside—like a door's being
knocked down.* DUBBA J *drops to the floor and begins to crawl. He
crawls behind the candy counter. Outside police helicopter searchlights track across the patio and courtyard. The sound of a police
helicopter overhead gets louder and louder.*

Something draws DUBBA J *from his hiding place. He goes outside on
the patio.*

*The sound of police dogs barking enters the courtyard. Helicopter
searchlights track around him. Paper and small debris swirl around
him.*

DUBBA J *looks up to the heavens. A search light shines down on him.*
DUBBA J *stands isolated in a pool of light, with darkness all around.
A moment of dread. Abrupt Blackout.*

END OF ACT ONE

ACT TWO – SCENE ONE

Over two hours later.

The candy house is wrecked. Absolutely trashed. Anywhere the police thought drugs might be hidden was searched and torn apart, including the Wall of Fame. Broken frames and pictures cover the candy table. Glass covers that. All the candy boxes are empty. Candy covers the floor. Many candies like M&M's, Skittles, and Reese's Pieces and all of the chips are out of their wrappers. Basically anything that could hide drugs was torn into—making the floor a crunchy, sticky mess.

The kitchen is a wreck, too. The business fridge is wide open, most of its contents confiscated.

When lights come up, JON-JON *stands at the sliding glass door. He peeks out the blinds.*

ROSE *sits against the candy counter. She plays jacks.*

Every now and then the sound of a helicopter is heard and a searchlight tracks outside.

ROSE

Jon-Jon! Told you to get away from the door. Shit.

(He doesn't move)

What I say?

(He moves away from the door. He sits down)

And take your ass to the door one more time. Hardheaded. Come here. Sit by me.

(A beat. He just stares at her. Then he turns his back to her)

Alright. Be hardheaded.

(A lull of silence. JON-JON *keeps looking at the sliding glass door. She keeps playing jacks. This goes on for a spell, then* JON-JON *looks back at her—to size up his chances to escape—but* ROSE *is onto him. He ain't slick)*

Why you looking at me all hard?

JON-JON

What are you doing?

ROSE

I'm playing jacks. What it look like I'm doing?

JON-JON

You're a grown-ass woman.

ROSE

I'm gonna tell your parents how you talk when they're not around. Watch that mouth. Being mannish. And don't look at me like that. I carry these on me for times like these. I find me a private spot where I can be alone and I play. It calms my nerves. Gets my head right.

(Beat)

And I'm not used to being stared at when I do it. It's rude to stare.

(Quiet. She goes back to playing. She finds her zen place for a moment. This is JON-JON*'s chance. Slowly he begins to scoot over. He gets almost there—when she catches him)*

JON-JON! Get away from the window. The police come through and see you in that window. They say they thought you was trying to ambush them. Your ass be dead. And the Bloods see you, they come fucking with us. I'm trying to keep it together. But I need you to sit down and be still. Come over here. Sit by me. If you sit down, it will relax your nerves. 'Aight. And before you know it mama and daddy will come walking through that door.

*(*JON-JON *goes and sits next to* ROSE*)*
See. Don't that feel better?

JON-JON *doesn't answer.*
She goes back to playing jacks. A long moment passes.

JON-JON

Why they not back yet? The police took them to jail. I know it.

ROSE

Mama and daddy gonna be fine. Don't say that.

JON-JON

Why they put them in the back of police cars?

ROSE

They're just asking them questions.

JON-JON

Why can't they ask them questions on the streets? Why they sitting in police cars?

109

ROSE

They have to get them alone. One-on-one.

JON-JON

Why?

ROSE

'Cause that's what they do.

JON-JON

But why / they—

ROSE

Your parents ain't going to jail!
Aight! They're not criminals. They haven't done anything wrong.

JON-JON

We hid your drugs.

ROSE

I got all the drugs back. There's no drugs in the candy house.

JON-JON

But the police lady / said—

ROSE

What police lady?

JON-JON

The police lady that walked me back to the candy house. Before
you came.

ROSE

What did the police lady say?

JON-JON

That mama and daddy could be in trouble.

ROSE

Jon-Jon, trust me. There were no drugs for the police to find. I
mean that. Square business. Your parents not in any trouble.

 (Beat)

And your ass shouldn't be out here no way. Shit. Who brings a
twelve-year-old to a drug bust?

JON-JON

We didn't know it was a drug bust. We didn't know what was going
on. Mama heard some explosions on the phone. And then daddy
didn't come back on the line. So we come here looking for him.

ROSE

She should have left you at home.

JON-JON

But I wanted to come see 'bout daddy.

ROSE

This ain't no place for you. It's like a battle zone and shit. That li'l
girl died and all hell broke loose.

JON-JON

What li'l girl?

The girl that got shot at the swimming pool.

JON-JON

She died?

ROSE

Your mama didn't tell you? Yeah. It's fucked up.
And that's another reason why your ass don't need to be out here.
Stupid letting you come.

JON-JON

My mama not stupid. You're stupid.

ROSE

I didn't mean it like that.

JON-JON *turns away from her. Shuts her out. A beat or two passes.*

JON-JON

Daddy said she wasn't gonna die.

ROSE

Jon-Jon.

(*He doesn't look at her*)

Jon-Jon.

(*Nothing*)

Jon-Jon! I got something for you.

He turns to look. She holds the jacks out for him to take.

It'll make you feel better. I promise.

JON-JON

Boys don't play jacks.
And neither do drug dealers.

She goes back to playing.

ROSE

I don't care what you say. It's good for the soul.

JON-JON

Kingston know you play jacks?

ROSE

Nobody knows I play jacks. Except for you. And it better stay that way.

(JON-JON*'s attention goes back to the sliding glass door. She grabs his arm)*

Don't even think about it.

(Beat)

I'm sorry. How's your hand?

A beat. JON-JON *doesn't answer at first.*

JON-JON

Fine.

ROSE

You sure?

JON-JON

Ain't that what I said?

ROSE

Little boy, don't play with me.

(Beat)

Move it around. Do something with your hand so I can know its
okay?

(JON-JON *gives her the finger*)

Stop that!

Mama was right about you. Your little mannish ass need Jesus. Shit
I'd drive you to the goddamn Vacation Bible School my damn self
if I had a car.

JON-JON

How is it you sell drugs but you can't afford a car?

ROSE

I can afford a car. Shit. I can afford two cars if I wanted. I just
choose to invest my money someplace else. And you need to stay
outta grown-folks' business.

Silence for a few beats.

JON-JON

Is that your stomach? You hungry?

ROSE

Yeah.

JON-JON

You're always thinking about food.

ROSE

Everybody got their vices. You know what I been having a taste for?
Fried turkey. Daddy needs to start selling fried turkey.

JON-JON

That would be too expensive. They don't sell turkey under the
bridge too often. Only in November and December. Sometimes not
even then.

ROSE

What bridge?

JON-JON

The bridge daddy buys all the meat from in South Dallas.

ROSE

Wait. He feeding us meat he bought under a bridge?

JON-JON

Uh-huh.

ROSE

You're playing with me.

                              JON-JON
Nope.

                               ROSE
Bullshit.

                              JON-JON
I bullshit you not.

                               ROSE
How do he know that meat FDA-approved?

                              JON-JON
This coming from a drug dealer.

                               ROSE
Don't try and change the subject—and I'm an entrepreneur.

                              JON-JON
Well my daddy an entrepreneur too.

                               ROSE
You didn't have to insult me.

                              JON-JON
I was just stating fact.

        There is knocking at the sliding glass door. They don't answer.

                              NICOLE
Jon-Jon. It's Nicky. You in there?

ROSE *opens the door and grabs* NICOLE *and yanks her in.*

ROSE

What the fuck is your problem? Strolling around like fucking Anne of Green Gables or some shit. You see them dudes out there?

NICOLE

I took my chances.

(*Goes to* JON-JON. *Wraps him in her arms*)

Baby, are you okay? What's happening?

ROSE

The police separated his parents. They being questioned in the parking lot.

NICOLE

Yeah, I saw that. And I was talking to Jon-Jon. Oh baby. Everything gonna be alright. Nicky here. You wanna come back to my place? Wait on your parents there?

ROSE

No. It's not safe. You can't go outside.

JON-JON

She won't let me leave.

NICOLE

What?

JON-JON

I tried to leave and she grabbed me. And she cussed at me. She hurt
my hand.

NICOLE

What that fuck is your problem?

ROSE

He yanked away from me. That's how his hand got hurt.

JON-JON

Like she tried to pull it real hard. Almost broke my wrist.

ROSE

No. No. It was an accident.

NICOLE

How you like it if I broke your wrist?

ROSE	JON-JON
IT WAS AN ACCIDENT.	It still hurts.

JON-JON

I don't wanna be here no more. I wanna see my mama and daddy.

ROSE

Li'l dude. Dude . . .

NICOLE

Don't touch him. Get away.

JON-JON

I don't wanna be here.

He makes a run for the sliding glass door. ROSE *gets ahead of him and blocks it.*

ROSE

I SAID NO!

JON-JON *turns and runs to the front door.*

ROSE	NICOLE
Shit!	Jon-Jon!

JON-JON *opens the front door. He sees something outside. He yells out in fear. And slams the door. He runs to the bathroom and hides.*

ROSE *gestures for* NICOLE *to be quiet. She pulls out her gun and goes to the door to look out the peephole.*

NICOLE

What's going—

ROSE *shushes* NICOLE.

NICOLE

(Under her breath)
Get away from that glass. Just be quiet.

ROSE

(NICOLE *moves away from the sliding glass door. Quiet for a tense spell. Then* ROSE *looks out the peephole again)*

119

ROSE (*Cont'd*)

Yeah, that's right. Walk the fuck away.

NICOLE

Who was it?

ROSE

Two Bloods.

NICOLE

The gang?

ROSE

You know about them?

NICOLE

Yeah. They used to be at Shantay's old place. That's why she had to move.

ROSE

Well they picked the wrong muthafuckas this time.

NICOLE

If the police out, how come they roaming around like it ain't nothing?

ROSE

The Bloods don't give a fuck about nothing. That's why they dangerous and that's why we can't let them take over. Killing some innocent li'l girl. Just spraying bullets for no reason. We don't do shit like that.

*(She looks out the peephole again. Looks like coast is clear. She goes
to the bathroom door and knocks)*

Jon-Jon, it's okay. They're gone. You can come out now.

*(*JON-JON *stays put)*

I scared them away. I have my gun. I won't let nobody hurt you.
Jon-Jon.

(No response from JON-JON*)*

How do you talk a kid out of a locked room? I know how to get a
crackhead out of a locked room. But . . . this is . . . different. Nicky?
Any suggestions?

NICOLE

I don't know.

ROSE

You got a kid.

NICOLE

Tamera ain't at that age yet. Thank God.

ROSE *gives up. She looks out the peephole again, then she finds a
broom and begins to sweep up some of the mess. Quiet for a beat
while she sweeps.* NICOLE *just stares at her.*

ROSE

I'd 'preciate some help.

NICOLE

Whatchu doing that for?

ROSE

Don't want mama to see the place like this.

NICOLE

She not gonna care. They not staying.

ROSE

Whatchu mean?

NICOLE

After tonight. The candy house is done. Don't you know that? Save
yourself the trouble.

ROSE *keeps sweeping.*

ROSE

I don't like seeing the candy house this way.

NICOLE

Knock yourself out then.

ROSE *sweeps. Trying to sort and organize debris along the way. But
after a bit she stops. She was just bullshitting about needing order.
She grabs the jacks.*

ROSE

Onesies or twosies?

NICOLE

I thought you was cleaning?

ROSE

I asked you a question. Onesies or twosies?

NICOLE

Onesies.

ROSE

Onesies? Since when?

NICOLE

I'm not in the mood.

ROSE

You can stay here and play jacks with your homegirl or you can tear
your ass. Take your chances with the Bloods.

NICOLE

Twosies.

ROSE

That's more like it.

(They play jacks with ROSE *'s gun sitting in the middle)*
You miss Tamera?

NICOLE

That's a stupid question.

ROSE

You should be able to bring her home by tomorrow night.

NICOLE

How you know?

ROSE

Kingston say he working on a plan. He gonna run the Bloods out.
They not gonna fuck with our neighborhood no more. He gonna
make it quiet again, so five-oh will leave our ass alone. It's gonna be
real nice, like it always been.

(Beat)

You got a gun at home?

NICOLE

What?

ROSE

Do you have a gun at home?

NICOLE

You said it was gonna be cool again. Why I need a gun?

ROSE

On general principle. GP. Hell, what you think? You a single mother with a little girl. You need a gun.

NICOLE

Yes. I have a gun.

ROSE

What kind?

NICOLE

A pistol.

ROSE

A Glock pistol?

NICOLE

I don't know. I think it's just a regular pistol . . . I guess.

ROSE *stops playing.*

ROSE

You don't know what kind of gun you have?

(NICOLE *shrugs her shoulders)*

What kind of ammo you use?

NICOLE

Bullets . . . ?
I don't know, it's a gun. It was a hand-me-down.

ROSE

A hand-me-down gun?

NICOLE

It belonged to my granny.

ROSE

It ain't the same gun she pulled on Kareem when she found out he had got you pregnant?

NICOLE

Yeah.

ROSE

That old thing!
Girl, you need a better gun than that.

NICOLE

Like what?

ROSE

Like this. Like mine. I can get you one. No cost. I'll even teach you
how to use it.

NICOLE

My pistol is fine.

ROSE

Might wanna reconsider.
    (A beat. They continue to play)
Why you keep looking at it?

NICOLE

It looks heavy.

ROSE

Yeah.
Wanna hold it?
    (NICOLE *hesitates. Then she reaches for the gun. Then relents.*
    Unsure)

Don't worry. Change your mind, you know where to find me.

(They continue to play in silence for a beat)

Nicky . . .

NICOLE

Yeah?

ROSE

I'm sorry 'bout Marcus.
I just been meaning to say.

NICOLE

You don't owe me an apology.

ROSE

Feels like I do.

NICOLE

It was easier to blame you. But it wasn't your fault. It was his.

A beat. Then another beat.

ROSE

When was the last time you visited?

NICOLE

I haven't.

ROSE

Not at all?

(Beat)

He's gonna be mad.

NICOLE

I don't care. He fucked our lives.

(Beat)

He writes my sister. Trying to get to me.

(Beat)

I know it's wrong not to visit. I'm just afraid.

ROSE

Afraid of what?

NICOLE *shrugs her shoulders.*

NICOLE

Tamera doesn't really understand.

ROSE

I'm here if you need to talk.

NICOLE

Thanks.

I worry about you ending up like Marcus.

ROSE

I won't.

NICOLE

Better not.

ROSE *nods her head. They don't know what else to say. Quiet again.
They play. Then . . . a sound outside.*

ROSE

(Whispers)
Somebody outside.

ROSE *goes to the sliding glass door to check.*

KINGSTON

Rosie!
(She opens the sliding glass door. KINGSTON *comes inside and sees
the damage)*
BUMBOCLAAT!

KINGSTON *reaches back out to usher* LAURA MAE *into the candy house.*
DUBBA J *helps his wife in. She pulls away.*

LAURA MAE

BABY! IS MY BABY HERE!
*(*JON-JON *races out of the room and into his mother's arms)*
I was so scared! I was so scared! Had that dog on you. Sniffing you
like trash. I was so scared. They took you away. I ain't know what
to think.

KINGSTON

Mommy. Sit down. Rest.

She doesn't. She scans the room.

DUBBA J

Laura Mae / baby—

She waves him off. She is overwhelmed.

LAURA MAE

My Lord! My Lord!

(She collapses. KINGSTON *catches her to help her into a chair)*

I wanna go home. I wanna go home.

KINGSTON

Mommy, everything criss. I take care of everything. Don't cry. Get mommy somewhere to sit. Don't stand around. Bumboraas! Do something! You too, pupa! You see mommy not happy.

*(*JON-JON *grabs a folding chair for his mother.* KINGSTON *helps her into it.* ROSE *gets her some tap water. She gulps it down.* KINGSTON *barks out orders to the whole room)*

Made mi stomach turn seeing mommy in the back of that police car like a bloodclaat animal.

(To NICOLE*)*

What you look at me like that for. We settle our business. Eh? You gonna stand there and look stupid or you going to help?

NICOLE

Let me take her to the back room. So she can rest. Doctor on you a bit. Okay?

LAURA MAE

No. I wanna go home.

ROSE

It's not safe to leave.

KINGSTON

You stay here for the night.

LAURA MAE

No. No.

DUBBA J

Laura Mae, they right. Wait till daylight.

LAURA MAE

I wanna go home!

DUBBA J

What if the police follow us back to Red Oak? Do to our house what they did to this place? What if them boys follow us?

NICOLE

The Bloods?

DUBBA J

Yeah.
Cookie. I'm sorry. But we gotta wait till day.

LAURA MAE *begins to whimper.*

131

NICOLE

Ssssssssssssssh, just relax. Come with me.

DUBBA J

Son. You alright?

JON-JON *just stares at his dad for a beat. Then he goes with his mom
and* NICOLE.

KINGSTON *and* ROSE *walk around the room surveying the damage.*

KINGSTON

Can anything be salvaged?

(ROSE *scoops up candy crumbs in her hand, then lets them pour out
like sand)*

The fuckery! Two-faced bastard.

ROSE

Was it the black cop with the mole / over—

DUBBA J

Yeah, that ugly muthafucka. Same one from yesterday. He wanna
fuck with me. Come on with it. But he leave my wife alone.

KINGSTON

(To ROSE*)*

Go in the room with mommy.

(He waits until she is gone)

Shame. We got to do something, pupa. How much?

DUBBA J

How much?

KINGSTON

How much it cost to put this place back together? I need a number.

DUBBA J

Now?

KINGSTON

Yeah. Now.
You're not giving up, are you? Don't let the police scare you. I don't want to tink about the neighborhood without the candy house. We ying and yang. Let me put it another way. How much it cost to keep you here?

DUBBA J

I don't have a number.

KINGSTON

A thousand dollars.

DUBBA J

You serious?

KINGSTON

A month. I pay you a thousand dollars a month to stay.

DUBBA J

You put me on your payroll? Naw. Naw. I don't like the sound of that.

KINGSTON

It's not a payroll. Just taking care of you like family do. I do the same ting for my family back home. What mi people eat and drink come out of that. Just paying in advance.

DUBBA J

I can't take that money.

KINGSTON

I want you to have this. I want to help. This is my fault. I want to make tings right.
    (Beat)
If the candy house go away, then this neighborhood will be like all the other places you see on TV.

DUBBA J

Shit. We already on the goddamn television.

KINGSTON

But we had nothing to do with that. But if you shut these doors then the next time will be all your fault. And there will be a next time. Believe me. If you close the candy house then I leave too. I'm not sticking 'round to see what happens next. Can you sleep with that?
    (Beat)
Pupa, I can make all our problems go away.

DUBBA J

How?

                    KINGSTON

Mi fight fiyah with fiyah.

                     DUBBA J

I don't want any more violence.

                    KINGSTON

I have to make it ugly.

   A beat.

                     DUBBA J

You gonna hurt innocent people?

                    KINGSTON

No. I never do.

   (DUBBA J *isn't convinced*)

I know how to handle these tings . . .

   (Beat)

I know a spot. Far from here.

                     DUBBA J

I ain't sign up for this shit. I don't want no parts.

                    KINGSTON

Pupa!

   DUBBA J *waves him off—becoming unsteady.*

                     DUBBA J

I need to sit down.

                        135

DUBBA J *(Cont'd)*
(KINGSTON *helps him into a chair)*
I don't feel so good.

KINGSTON

It never feels good. I get no pleasure. But we men of commerce.
We have to protect our interest. Don't let some fassyhole punks
ruin everything you've worked for. If I can make our troubles
pass—then you will stay? Yes, pupa?

A beat as DUBBA J *considers.* NICOLE *comes out of the bedroom. She
watches without being seen.*

DUBBA J

Yes.

KINGSTON

(Examines the weariness on DUBBA J*'s face)*
Pupa. Stop it. You bringing me down. I feel bad enough. Come on.
Take the money. It will cheer you up. So you had a shitty-ass day.
Let it come. Let it go. Ain't that what you said?

KINGSTON *notices* NICOLE *and backs off. He places the money on the
candy counter.*

NICOLE

I'm going home. Mama Laura say she wanna be alone.

DUBBA J

Is it safe?

NICOLE

Rose walking me.

KINGSTON

I can walk you home.

NICOLE

Really?

KINGSTON

Yeah. So we can talk.

NICOLE

Talk about what?

KINGSTON

I want to join the Neighborhood Watch.

NICOLE

I'd prefer Rose.

KINGSTON

I'm trying to be a friend. Your choice.

KINGSTON *leaves.* DUBBA J *and* NICOLE *stand in silence for a spell. Not sure what to say. Then* DUBBA J *picks the scraps of the petition off the floor.*

DUBBA J

If you got Scotch tape we can put it back together.

NICOLE

I can't take no busted up petitions down to city hall.

DUBBA J

Why not?

NICOLE

Because some shit you just don't do.

DUBBA J

Just say that a drug dealer ripped it out of your hands and tore it
to pieces. But you said "Fuck that, I'mma take this shit downtown
anyway." That'll make 'em think real highly of you.

NICOLE

But a drug dealer didn't tear it to pieces. You did.
   (A beat. DUBBA J *can't respond*)
Don't worry. I'm done with that. Somebody else can take it over.

DUBBA J

I've never known you to run from a fight.

NICOLE

I have to put my daughter first.

DUBBA J

I said the same thing 'bout Jon-Jon. Ain't work out how I thought.

NICOLE

Look like it worked out for you pretty good.

DUBBA J

What you mean?

NICOLE

I'm not stupid. I know what I saw. If he can get to you, he can
get to anybody. Shit already changing. Folks changing. Folks you
thought you knew.

DUBBA J

Tape these up. Rub something red on it. Make it look like blood
and shit. Put on a good show for city hall. Shed a few crocodile
tears. You know what to do.

NICOLE

What you gonna do about that money? You gonna keep it?

(Beat. DUBBA J doesn't answer. NICOLE is done)

Hey Rose. I'm ready.

ROSE comes out. NICOLE dumps the petition and leaves with her.

DUBBA J is tired and sits. A few beats pass. LAURA MAE comes out.

LAURA MAE

We alone?

DUBBA J

I thought you were sleeping.

LAURA MAE

Dubba J . . . Can't sleep . . .

(Beat)

Wait . . . Where's your wedding ring? The police take it?

(A beat. Fuck. DUBBA J *considers his answer)*

Dubba J?

DUBBA J

Baby I can't think straight right now.

(Beat)

Cookie. Baby. I'm sorry.

LAURA MAE

Sorry about what?

DUBBA J

. . . Last week . . . I got robbed. Some sick, evil muthafucka, didn't have no weapon but he scared me so bad. Just caught me off guard. Took my wedding ring. But Kingston came in and ran him off 'fore it could get worse. He saved my life. I been wearing a fake ring until Kingston could find the real one.

LAURA MAE

Why you just now telling me this?

DUBBA J

Cookie, I was trying not to upset you. Didn't want you to worry.

LAURA MAE

I don't believe that.

DUBBA J

I'm trying to tell you the truth. I could have lied to you.

LAURA MAE

You been lying to me this whole damn time. If I knew about that robbery I never would have let Jon-Jon come back to the candy house. Ever. Shit, I would have made you shut this place down. But you knew this whole time and never said one muthafucking word. You hid that shit from me on purpose just so you could keep this goddamn candy house.

DUBBA J

Dammit, Cookie. I fucked up. I admit that. But I don't need this right now. So much shit going through my head and I'm trying to figure it out as fast as I can.

   (Beat)

I saw them police take Jon-Jon and that was the end of the world. Can't get that outta my head. And now you coming at me . . . I fucked up bad. But just give me a chance. I'm trying to make things right.

LAURA MAE

I don't think you know how to do that anymore.

A beat. LAURA MAE *leaves* DUBBA J *standing alone.*

DUBBA J *starts to follow but she slams the door. Outside some guys are laughing and making noise in the background.* DUBBA J *cuts off the lights. Darkness.*

End of Scene.

ACT TWO – SCENE TWO

Daybreak peeks through the blinds. DUBBA J *sleeps against the candy counter.*

After a moment, he wakes. Time to go. He checks on the family in the other room. They're sleeping. He comes back out. Looks out the peephole, then opens the door to check outside. Then he goes back to check the patio. He peeks through the blinds. He sees something and hurries out on the patio. He comes back with DONNIE, *helping his friend inside.*

> DUBBA J

What the hell you doing out there?

> DONNIE

Don't know.

> DUBBA J

What you mean you don't know?
> (DONNIE *pushes him away*)

Brother, you okay?

> DONNIE

I look okay to you? They got my boy.

> JON-JON

Who . . .

DONNIE

The police.

Two o'clock this morning. There was banging on our front door. It
was our neighbor, Dynetta. She said the police had Jr. right outside
the front gates here. Me and Juanita went down and they had my
boy and some other boys. Police wouldn't let us get to him . . . they
just put him in the back of a van . . .
And drove off . . . just like that . . . with our boy.

DUBBA J

He just a kid. They can't do nothing to 'im.

DONNIE

They arrested him, didn't they?

DUBBA J

Yeah / but he's too young—

DONNIE

He's sixteen. He turn seventeen in two days. My brother-in-law say
they gonna treat him like an adult.

DUBBA J

Fuck what he say. He don't know everything.

DONNIE

Tell Juanita that.

DUBBA J

How she holding up?

(DONNIE doesn't answer)

DUBBA J *(Cont'd)*

Why you not with her?

DONNIE

We had a fight. She kicked me out.

DUBBA J

She just hurt. Whatever she said, she didn't mean it.

DONNIE

She meant it. Every word. And she was right. Every word.

DUBBA J

Don't blame yourself, brother.

DONNIE

Gotta blame somebody. Who you say we blame?

DUBBA J

. . . y'all got a lawyer?

DONNIE

We working on it.

DUBBA J

You heard from Jr. yet?

DONNIE

We been calling the jail. Somebody on the phone at Lew Sterrett said they was gonna check to see if he been processed. Then we got disconnected. Couldn't get back through. That's when her brother started getting Juanita all wound up. That's when we started fighting.

DUBBA J

Is it her brother that works downtown at the courthouse?

DONNIE

Yeah, the office manager. Act like he know every goddamn thing.
  (Beat)
He say they giving out five years over a few . . . chunks.

DUBBA J

You think Don Jr. had something on / him—

DONNIE

What the hell you think? I gotta get out of here.

DUBBA J

Where you going?

DONNIE

What you care?

DUBBA J

You going back home? How much you drink?

DONNIE

Enough.

DUBBA J

You don't need to go back to the house if you been drinking too much. And if her brother still there, it ain't gonna be a good situation if you drunk.

DONNIE

I almost punched him in the face.

DUBBA J

Yeah. That's the shit I'm talking 'bout.

DONNIE *walks around looking at all the damage.*

DONNIE

This place look how I feel.

DONNIE *continues to sift through things. He makes his way over to the pictures. He finds something.*

DUBBA J

What is it?

DONNIE

It's nothing.

DUBBA J

Naw. I wanna see.

DONNIE *hands the picture to* DUBBA J.

DONNIE

Remember when our boys played football together?

DUBBA J

Yeah, I remember when you made Jon-Jon the goddamn water boy.

DONNIE

Well hell, he wasn't supposed to be on the team in the first place.
He wasn't even in the right age bracket. I could've got in trouble
behind that shit.

DUBBA J

Well why you put him on the team?

DONNIE

'Cause you asked me to. Wouldn't nobody else put the boy on a
team.

DUBBA J

Well you could've let him play once or twice, when the other teams
put their shitty-ass players out.

DONNIE

I didn't have no choice. Hell, I couldn't put Jon-Jon on the field.
The other boys would have killed him. Shit, he got the wind
knocked out of him—twice. And one of those times, he was sitting
on the bench.

DONNIE *laughs.* DUBBA J *laughs too.*

DUBBA J

But that boy of yours sho could run the ball.

DONNIE

Sho' could! Sometimes he ran it in the wrong direction. But goddammit—

DONNIE and DUBBA J

HE RAN THAT MUTHAFUCKA!

They laugh. And laugh. And laugh. Then DONNIE *'s laughter quickly
turns into a long sob.* DUBBA J *holds his friend, not knowing what to
say. After a beat,* DONNIE *moves away from* DUBBA J, *needing some
space.*

DUBBA J

Donnie. Brother, I'm sorry. I didn't know how bad it was . . . I just
thought . . . you know. Don Jr. was just being a knucklehead. You
know how boys get at that age. I didn't know what it all meant. I
didn't know how bad all this was gonna get. Didn't know what it all
was. You gotta believe me. I would have done different if I knew. I
promise you.

DONNIE

Yeah?

(A beat. JON-JON *comes out of the bedroom. He listens. They don't
see him)*

Last time I saw him, we had a fight. I kicked him out of the house.
Thought it'd scare some sense into him. Where the fuck he got to
go? He ain't gon' do shit but come right back home. Juanita begged

me not to do it. But I took his shit and I threw it out on the front porch. I just knew he'd come running back . . . home . . .

JON-JON

Mr. Donnie. Where's Don Jr.?

DONNIE *tries to hold it together, but can't. He hurries out of the candy house.*

DUBBA J

Brother . . . DONNIE!

JON-JON

What happened?

A beat.

DUBBA J

Don Jr. got arrested.

JON-JON

He's in jail? You could have done something.

DUBBA J

I'm sorry.

JON-JON

Too late to be sorry. It can't help nobody now. You didn't do anything. The last day of school we were in the car on the way to the candy house. I saw Don Jr. hanging on the corner with them boys. I pointed him out to you. But you didn't stop. You just kept going.

DUBBA J

I didn't wanna stop with you in the car.

JON-JON

Why?
   (DUBBA J *can't answer because the reason is too painful*)
Were you afraid like mama said?
Then you could have at least called his parents. Did you do that?

DUBBA J

No.

JON-JON

How are you gonna fix it?

DUBBA J

I don't know.

There is a knock at the front door.

KINGSTON

Pupa, it's me!

DUBBA J *gestures for* JON-JON *to be quiet. More knocking.*

KINGSTON

Pupa! Pupa! Open up!
   (*They remain quiet. More knocking*)
I know you're in there.
   (*Now banging at the sliding glass door*)

I'm not leaving until you open this door.

(They stand in silence for what feels like forever)

PUPA!

> DUBBA J *gestures for* JON-JON *to go back to the bedroom. He does. He lets* KINGSTON *in.*

DUBBA J

Sssssssssssssssh. All that noise. The family still sleep.

KINGSTON

Congratulate me. I got real good news.

DUBBA J

Good news?

KINGSTON

I brought the pleasant back to Pleasant Grove.

DUBBA J

Whatchu do?

KINGSTON

No worries. The less you know. The better. Mi boys coming by soon. Help clean up the candy house.

DUBBA J

I won't be here. Taking my family home.

KINGSTON

Yeah. But you coming back?

DUBBA J

Kingston, this gotta be the end of the line for me.

KINGSTON

But why? I fixed it.
We come too far to abandon everything we worked for.

DUBBA J

What do you mean *we*?

KINGSTON

We. WE! We men of commerce! Partners.

DUBBA J

Now look. Let's get something straight here. I've always respected
you. Always considered you a friend and a good neighbor. That's
always been the extent of it. But my business and your business has
always been separate.

KINGSTON

Wah gwaan? Pupa. You para' that's all.

DUBBA J

Kingston . . .
This ain't for me.

KINGSTON

Fine. Walk away and let your son / know—

DUBBA J

My son deserves better than this.

A beat.

KINGSTON

Go home, relax yourself. But you coming back to the candy house.

(KINGSTON *smiles. Extends his hand for a shake.* DUBBA J *doesn't accept*)

Pupa, take my hand. I don't want things to change.

(A beat. Standoff)

You gave me your word.

(ROSE *comes in through sliding glass door*)

Where you been?

ROSE

I got sick.

KINGSTON

Eh? That made you sick?

ROSE

Yeah.

(She starts for the bathroom. He blocks her)

I need to go to the bathroom.

KINGSTON

Yeah. You don't look so good. Splash some water on your face.

(He starts out. Then stops)

Eh.

He whispers something to her. She hands her gun over and hurries into the bathroom. After a few beats she sneaks into the bedroom when no one is watching.

DUBBA J

Why you take her gun?

KINGSTON

There are rules we have to follow.

DUBBA J

I don't follow those kinds of rules.

KINGSTON

You been following mi rules all this time.

DUBBA J

What the fuck that mean?

KINGSTON

You take care of my boys. You feed them.

DUBBA J

They're my customers like any other customers.

KINGSTON

You let them wait in here when the police come.

DUBBA J

They come in to buy candies and shit.

KINGSTON

They come in to hide. You protect them.

DUBBA J

I don't protect them.

KINGSTON

You let them stand on your patio and do their business.

DUBBA J

Now that's a goddamn lie.

KINGSTON

You don't be seeing them on your patio?

LAURA MAE, ROSE, *and* JON-JON *come out of the bedroom.* LAURA MAE *holds her son close for his safety.*

DUBBA J

Well hell yeah, I see 'em / but—

KINGSTON

You just look the other way. Like you supposed to do. You been doing good, pupa. Don't fuck up now.

(Beat)

Let me take Rose and be on my way.

DUBBA J

The first time I let Rosie walk out that door with you is one of the worst regrets of my life. She ain't come back the same Rosie I

155

remember. If I let her walk out that door with you today, she won't be coming back at all. Will she?

KINGSTON

Just stay out of it.

DUBBA J

I let my best friend's boy stand on that corner for you. And he won't be coming back the same.

KINGSTON

Pupa . . .

DUBBA J

Get out.
It's over. You have to go.

KINGSTON

Eh?

(DUBBA J *takes the money out of his pocket and puts it on the candy counter.*)

DUBBA J

Take that money and go.

KINGSTON

Pupa . . .

DUBBA J

Get out.

KINGSTON *stays put.*

LAURA MAE

My husband said get out.

KINGSTON

Mommy . . . ?

LAURA MAE

Don't play that with me. I know who you are.
What you are.
Rose told me.
Set a boy on fire.

ROSE

Stripped him naked.
Doused him with gasoline . . . Set him on fire . . .
Made Kendrick shoot 'im in the head when he stopped screaming.
You made us watch.

LAURA MAE

Made them all watch that boy burn to death.

KINGSTON

He killed an innocent little girl. He gets what he gets. I have to
make it ugly. To spare more bloodshed.
    (Beat)
I didn't have a choice. I did it to protect us. You.
    (Points to JON-JON*)*
Him.

Mi do for you but nobody do for mi. I could have walked away. Mi go someplace else. Say fuck it. Fuck you. Damaged goods. Let the Bloods take over. You cry tears over a fassyhole punk and say fuck mi. Joke pon mi. Joke pon mi.

(*Beat. To* ROSE)

Once a snitch. Always a snitch. Eh, Rose?
You tell that to the police too?

ROSE *is shook.*

ROSE

I don't know what you're talking about. I swear.

KINGSTON

Then why were you hiding from me?

ROSE

If I was hiding from you why would I come back here?

KINGSTON

Mi nuh know. Wah mek yuh suh chupid.
Police found out tings that nobody know but you. How you explain that?

(*Beat*)

Rose. Come with me. Don't drag them into your shit. The longer you stay the worse you make it for them. You want that on you?

ROSE *takes a step.* LAURA MAE *grabs her arm.*

LAURA MAE

No.

JON-JON

IT WAS ME!
I'm the snitch!

(Everyone stops. A beat . . . Another beat . . .)

Police said mommy and daddy was going to jail. Please don't hurt
Rosie-Girl. It was me.

KINGSTON

. . . what did you tell the police?

JON-JON

That Kingston's not your real name. Your real name is Michael
Bustamante Edwards. Your mama call you Busta. I told the / police—

DUBBA J

(To JON-JON*)*

STOP!

KINGSTON

Do you know what this means?

A dreadful beat. Even KINGSTON *is numb-frozen in shock. Then . . .*
LAURA MAE *panics. Chaos.*
KINGSTON *is still frozen. Not sure what to do.*

DUBBA J

What does it mean?

DUBBA J *(cont'd)*

He made a mistake. He's a kid. But I'm the one that fucked up. You gonna be a coward and kill a little boy? Man, you better than that. Here. Take this money. And let us be.

> DUBBA J *picks up the money and holds it out for* KINGSTON. *A beat.* KINGSTON *knocks the money out of* DUBBA J*'s hand. He grabs* DUBBA J *by the collar.* DUBBA J *pushes him off. This infuriates* KINGSTON *more. He pulls out his knife and charges* DUBBA J. *The men struggle and somehow* DUBBA J *gets the upper hand. He pins* KINGSTON *against the candy counter with the knife to his throat.*

> LAURA MAE *begins to frantically, urgently mumble a prayer.*

> KINGSTON *closes his eyes. Ready for death. He begins to mumble his own prayer-chant.*

KINGSTON

One. Two. Three. Lawdamercy. The devil gonna kill me.

*(*LAURA MAE*'s prayers intensify)*

One. Two. Three. Lawdamercy. The devil gonna kill me.

DUBBA J

(It's too much for DUBBA J*)*

LAURA MAE!

> LAURA MAE *stops praying.*

KINGSTON

One. Two. Three. Lawdamercy. The devil gonna kill me.

One. Two. Three. Lawdamercy. The devil gonna kill me.

One. Two. Three. Lawdamercy. The devil gonna kill me.

    (LAURA MAE *hides her son's face so he can't see*)

One. Two. Three. Lawdamercy. The devil gonna kill me.

    (DUBBA J *is seconds away from cutting* KINGSTON*'s throat, then* JON-
JON *begins to cry. A cry that only a kid can make.* DUBBA J *looks at his
son. A beat.* DUBBA J *shoves* KINGSTON *to the ground. He stands over
him ready in case* KINGSTON *attacks. Slowly,* KINGSTON *stands to his
feet. The two men stare look at each other . . . then . . .)*

Pray you never see me again.

    KINGSTON *looks at* ROSE. *A moment passes between them. Then she
races out of the candy house.*

    A beat. KINGSTON *takes one last look at the family. Then he leaves.*

    The family embraces. Slowly they pull away. Time to go.

    LAURA MAE *leaves with her son.*

    DUBBA J *stands in the doorway, alone. He takes one last look at the
candy house.*

    Then he slams the door shut.

    Abrupt blackout.

END OF PLAY

Thank you all
for your support.
We do this for you,
and could not do
it without you.

PARTNERS

pixel ||| texel

EMBREY FAMILY
FOUNDATION

ADDITIONAL DONORS, CONT'D

Mark Haber
Mary Cline
Maynard Thomson
Michael Reklis
Mike Soto
Mokhtar Ramadan
Nikki & Dennis Gibson
Patrick Kukucka
Patrick Kutcher
Rev. Elizabeth & Neil Moseley
Richard Meyer

Scott & Katy Nimmons
Sherry Perry
Sydneyann Binion
Stephen Harding
Stephen Williamson
Susan Carp
Susan Ernst
Theater Jones
Tim Perttula
Tony Thomson

SUBSCRIBERS

Joseph Rebella
Michael Lighty
Shelby Vincent
Margaret Terwey
Ben Fountain
Ryan Todd
Gina Rios
Elena Rush
Courtney Sheedy
Caroline West

Ned Russin
Laura Gee
Valerie Boyd
Brian Bell
Charles Dee Mitchell
Cullen Schaar
Harvey Hix
Jeff Lierly
Elizabeth Simpson
Michael Schneiderman

Nicole Yurcaba
Sam Soule
Jennifer Owen
Melanie Nicholls
Alan Glazer
Michael Doss
Matt Bucher
Katarzyna Bartoszynska
Anthony Brown
Elif Ağanoğlu

AVAILABLE NOW FROM DEEP VELLUM

MICHÈLE AUDIN · *One Hundred Twenty-One Days* · translated by Christiana Hills · FRANCE

BAE SUAH · *Recitation* · translated by Deborah Smith · SOUTH KOREA

MARIO BELLATIN · *Mrs. Murakami's Garden* · translated by Heather Cleary · MEXICO

EDUARDO BERTI · *The Imagined Land* · translated by Charlotte Coombe · ARGENTINA

CARMEN BOULLOSA · *Texas: The Great Theft* · *Before* · *Heavens on Earth*
translated by Samantha Schnee · Peter Bush · Shelby Vincent · MEXICO

MAGDA CARNECI · *FEM* · translated by Sean Cotter · ROMANIA

LEILA S. CHUDORI · *Home* · translated by John H. McGlynn · INDONESIA

MATHILDE CLARK · *Lone Star* · translated by Martin Aitken · DENMARK

SARAH CLEAVE, ed. · *Banthology: Stories from Banned Nations* ·
IRAN, IRAQ, LIBYA, SOMALIA, SUDAN, SYRIA & YEMEN

LOGEN CURE · *Welcome to Midland: Poems* · USA

ANANDA DEVI · *Eve Out of Her Ruins* · translated by Jeffrey Zuckerman · MAURITIUS

PETER DIMOCK · *Daybook from Sheep Meadow* · USA

CLAUDIA ULLOA DONOSO · *Little Bird*, translated by Lily Meyer · PERU/NORWAY

ROSS FARRAR · *Ross Sings Cheree & the Animated Dark: Poems* · USA

ALISA GANIEVA · *Bride and Groom* · *The Mountain and the Wall*
translated by Carol Apollonio · RUSSIA

FERNANDA GARCIA LAU · *Out of the Cage* · translated by Will Vanderhyden · ARGENTINA

ANNE GARRÉTA · *Sphinx* · *Not One Day* · *In/concrete* · translated by Emma Ramadan · FRANCE

JÓN GNARR · *The Indian* · *The Pirate* · *The Outlaw* · translated by Lytton Smith · ICELAND

GOETHE · *The Golden Goblet: Selected Poems* · *Faust, Part One*
translated by Zsuzsanna Ozsváth and Frederick Turner · GERMANY

NOEMI JAFFE · *What are the Blind Men Dreaming?* · translated by Julia Sanches & Ellen Elias-Bursac · BRAZIL

CLAUDIA SALAZAR JIMÉNEZ · *Blood of the Dawn* · translated by Elizabeth Bryer · PERU

PERGENTINO JOSÉ · *Red Ants* · MEXICO

TAISIA KITAISKAIA · *The Nightgown & Other Poems* · USA

JUNG YOUNG MOON · *Seven Samurai Swept Away in a River* · *Vaseline Buddha*
translated by Yewon Jung · SOUTH KOREA

KIM YIDEUM · *Blood Sisters* · translated by Ji yoon Lee · SOUTH KOREA

JOSEFINE KLOUGART · *Of Darkness* · translated by Martin Aitken · DENMARK

YANICK LAHENS · *Moonbath* · translated by Emily Gogolak · HAITI

FOUAD LAROUI · *The Curious Case of Dassoukine's Trousers* · translated by Emma Ramadan · MOROCCO

MARIA GABRIELA LLANSOL · *The Geography of Rebels Trilogy: The Book of Communities; The Remaining Life; In the House of July & August* translated by Audrey Young · PORTUGAL

PABLO MARTÍN SÁNCHEZ · *The Anarchist Who Shared My Name* · translated by Jeff Diteman · SPAIN

DOROTA MASŁOWSKA · *Honey, I Killed the Cats* · translated by Benjamin Paloff · POLAND

BRICE MATTHIEUSSENT· *Revenge of the Translator* · translated by Emma Ramadan · FRANCE

LINA MERUANE · *Seeing Red* · translated by Megan McDowell · CHILE

VALÉRIE MRÉJEN · *Black Forest* · translated by Katic Shireen Assef · FRANCE

FISTON MWANZA MUJILA · *Tram 83* · translated by Roland Glasser · DEMOCRATIC REPUBLIC OF CONGO

GORAN PETROVIĆ · *At the Lucky Hand, aka The Sixty-Nine Drawers* · translated by Peter Agnone · SERBIA

ILJA LEONARD PFEIJFFER · *La Superba* · translated by Michele Hutchison · NETHERLANDS

RICARDO PIGLIA · *Target in the Night* · translated by Sergio Waisman · ARGENTINA

SERGIO PITOL · *The Art of Flight* · *The Journey* · *The Magician of Vienna* · *Mephisto's Waltz: Selected Short Stories* translated by George Henson · MEXICO

JULIE POOLE · *Bright Specimen: Poems from the Texas Herbarium* · USA

EDUARDO RABASA · *A Zero-Sum Game* · translated by Christina MacSweeney · MEXICO

ZAHIA RAHMANI · *"Muslim": A Novel* · translated by Matthew Reeck · FRANCE/ALGERIA

JUAN RULFO · *The Golden Cockerel & Other Writings* · translated by Douglas J. Weatherford · MEXICO

ETHAN RUTHERFORD · *Farthest South & Other Stories* · USA

TATIANA RYCKMAN · *Ancestry of Objects* · USA

OLEG SENTSOV · *Life Went On Anyway* · translated by Uilleam Blacker · UKRAINE

MIKHAIL SHISHKIN · *Calligraphy Lesson: The Collected Stories* translated by Marian Schwartz, Leo Shtutin, Mariya Bashkatova, Sylvia Maizell · RUSSIA

ÓFEIGUR SIGURÐSSON · *Öræfi: The Wasteland* · translated by Lytton Smith · ICELAND

DANIEL SIMON, ED. · *Dispatches from the Republic of Letters* · USA

MUSTAFA STITOU · *Two Half Faces* · translated by David Colmer · NETHERLANDS

MÄRTA TIKKANEN · *The Love Story of the Century* · translated by Stina Katchadourian · SWEDEN

SERHIY ZHADAN · *Voroshilovgrad* · translated by Reilly Costigan-Humes & Isaac Wheeler · UKRAINE

FORTHCOMING FROM DEEP VELLUM

SHANE ANDERSON · *After the Oracle* · USA

MARIO BELLATIN · *Beauty Salon* · translated by David Shook · MEXICO

MIRCEA CĂRTĂRESCU · *Solenoid*
translated by Sean Cotter · ROMANIA

LEYLÂ ERBIL · *A Strange Woman*
translated by Nermin Menemencioğlu & Amy Marie Spangler· TURKEY

RADNA FABIAS · *Habitus* · translated by David Colmer · CURAÇAO/NETHERLANDS

SARA GOUDARZI · *The Almond in the Apricot* · USA

GYULA JENEI · *Always Different* · translated by Diana Senechal · HUNGARY

UZMA ASLAM KHAN • *The Miraculous True History of Nomi Ali* • PAKISTAN

SONG LIN · *The Gleaner Song: Selected Poems* · translated by Dong Li · CHINA

TEDI LÓPEZ MILLS · *The Book of Explanations* · translated by Robin Myers · MEXICO

JUNG YOUNG MOON · *Arriving in a Thick Fog*
translated by Mah Eunji and Jeffrey Karvonen · SOUTH KOREA

FISTON MWANZA MUJILA · *The Villain's Dance,* translated by Roland Glasser · *The River in the Belly: Selected Poems,* translated by Bret Maney · DEMOCRATIC REPUBLIC OF CONGO

LUDMILLA PETRUSHEVSKAYA · *Kidnapped: A Crime Story,* translated by Marian Schwartz · *The New Adventures of Helen: Magical Tales,* translated by Jane Bugaeva · RUSSIA

SERGIO PITOL · *The Love Parade* · translated by G. B. Henson · MEXICO

MANON STEFAN ROS · *The Blue Book of Nebo* · WALES

JIM SCHUTZE · *The Accommodation* · USA

SOPHIA TERAZAWA · *Winter Phoenix: Testimonies in Verse* · POLAND

BOB TRAMMELL · *Jack Ruby & the Origins of the Avant-Garde in Dallas & Other Stories* · USA

BENJAMIN VILLEGAS · *ELPASO: A Punk Story* · translated by Jay Noden · MEXICO